MARRIAGES *and* DEATHS

from

The York Recorder

1821-1830

F. Edward Wright

HERITAGE BOOKS
2008

HERITAGE BOOKS

AN IMPRINT OF HERITAGE BOOKS, INC.

Books, CDs, and more—Worldwide

For our listing of thousands of titles see our website
at
www.HeritageBooks.com

Published 2008 by
HERITAGE BOOKS, INC.
Publishing Division
100 Railroad Ave. #104
Westminster, Maryland 21157

Originally published by
Family Line Publications
1995

International Standard Book Numbers
Paperbound: 978-1-58549-007-3
Clothbound: 978-0-7884-7490-3

INTRODUCTION

The *York Recorder* was published by John Edie and Robert McClellan beginning in 1800. It was a continuation of the *Pennsylvania Herald and York General Advertiser* which had been started in 1789 by James and John Edie and Henry Wilcocks. *The Recorder* ended publication in 1830. Samuel Wagner was the last editor.

This volume of abstracts, made from the extant copies at the Library of Congress, covers the period beginning 6 January 1821 and running through 23 February 1830. Included are notices of marriages and deaths, whether they occurred in York County or the surrounding counties of Pennsylvania and Maryland.

Each issue of the newspaper is given a number, and the individual items appearing in that issue follow. Each item starts on a new line, making it easy to find an item.

Robert Barnes

THE YORK RECORDER, PENNSYLVANIA

1. Jan 6 1821 (Saturday)
Died at Durham, the 22d inst., John J. Kelly, age 20.
Married Sunday last by Rev. Mr. Miller, Benjamin Lanius to Miss
Elizabeth Ilgenfritz, dau. of Samuel Ilgenfritz, all of this borough.

2. Jan 13 1821 (Saturday) Died Tuesday night last, Mr. Jacob
Schultz Sr., of this borough, in his 52nd year.

3. Jan 20 1821 (Saturday) Died on the 14th inst. at the house of
Joseph Hemphill, Esq., in Philadelphia, Charles Hall, Esq., of
Sunbury, Counsellor at Law, in his 52nd year.

4. Jan 27 1821 (Saturday)
Married on Tuesday evening last by Rev. Mr. Schmucker, Mr. John
Preston to Miss Mary Leitner, dau. of Mr. George Leitner, of this
borough.
Died at Fredericktown on the 16th inst., Mr. Peter Hardt, of that
place.

5. Feb 3 1821 (Saturday)
Died on Saturday last, Mr. Job H. Faddis of Newholland, York Co.
- On the same day, Mr. Abraham Cremer, of Buttstown.
- On Friday morning 19th ult. at residence near Middletown, Dauphin
County, in his 29th year, George R. Hopkins, Esq., eldest son of
James Hopkins, Esq., of this city.
- In Philadelphia on Monday evening the 15th inst., of dropsy, Mr.
Adan Koenigmucher in his 42nd year.
- On Fri, the 19th, Thomas Willing, Esq., in his 80 year of age. He was
a respectable merchant and for many years President of the late
Bank of the United States.

6. Feb 10 1821 (Saturday)
Married on Tuesday evening last by Rev. Mr. Mayer, Mr. Jacob Hoke
of Harford County, Md., to Miss Eliza Spangler, dau. of Mr. Samuel
Spangler, merchant, of this borough.
Died yesterday, Mr. Lewis Fisher, of this borough.

7. Feb 17 1821 (Saturday) Married on Tuesday last by Rev. Mr. Schmucker, Mr. George Erwin to Miss Mary Sprenkle, both of York Township.

8. Mar 3 1821 (Saturday)
Married on Thurs, Feb 15th, by Rev. W. Stevenson, Mr. Stephen Boyd, of York County, Pa., to Miss Eliza Stump, of Harford County, Md.
Died at Harrisburg, on 28th ult., in his 65th year, Benjamin Foulerl, Esq., member of the House of Representatives, from Bucks County.
- At Waterloo, N.Y. Jan 30th, Mr. David Miller in his 57th year. He was village sexton for a number of years.

9. Apr 10 1821 (Tuesday)
Married at Sandy Mount, lately, by Rev. Aquilla Garretson, Mr. John Stockdale to Miss Sarah A. Kurtz, dau. of the late Jacob Kurtz, of Baltimore.
Died on the 4th inst., in Westmoreland County, William Findley in his 83d year.

10. Apr 17 1821 (Tuesday)
Married on Wednesday the 10th inst., at Columbia, by Rev. Mr. Boyer, Mr. Daniel Small, of this borough, to Miss Elizabeth Fisher, dau. of George Fisher, Esq., of Harrisburg.
Died on Thursday last in this borough, Mrs. Small, wife of Daniel Small, and dau. of Rev. Mr. Craver, of this place, in her 30th year.

11. Apr 24 1821 (Tuesday)
Married on Thursday week last, by Rev. Mr. Speck in Monaghan township, Mr. William Carr to Miss Elizabeth Gates.
- On Tuesday last by Rev. Constantine Miller, Mr. George Loucks, of Manchester township, to Miss Catharine Shank, dau. of George Shank, of West Manchester township.
- On Thursday last, in Fairview township, Mr. John Conrad to Miss Ann Moore.
Died on Wednesday morning last, Mr. John Eichelberger, tavern keeper of this borough in his 50th year.
- On the same day, Mr. George Pflieger, of Codorus township.

12. May 8 1821 (Tuesday)
Married at Lancaster on the 30th inst. by Rev. Mr. Clarkson, Mr.
  Samuel D. Orrick to Miss Caroline Ross, dau. of George Ross, Esq.,
- At the same place on Tuesday evening last, by Rev. Endreas, Mr.
  Charles Wetherill, of Philadelphia, to Miss Margaret Mayer, of
  Lancaster.
Died on Tuesday last, in this borough, Mr. John ----(?).
- On Thursday last, wide Barbara Lonius, of this place.
- On Wednesday last, at York Haven, Mr. George Poor, merchant.
- On Friday morning last, at Lewberry, at a very advanced age, Hannah
  Willis, wife of John Willis.

13. May 15 1821 (Tuesday)
Married at Baltimore Thursday evening last, by Rev. Tydings, Mr.
  George Downey of this borough to Miss Nancy Wall, 2nd dau. of Mr.
  Jacob Wall of the former place.
Died in Newbury township on Thursday morning, Adam Kister, Esq.

14. May 22 1821 (Tuesday)
Died in this borough on Sunday last, Mr. John Dobbins, in his 68th
  year.
- At Middletown, on Friday the 11th inst., Elisha Green, Esq., in his
  56th year, a Magistrate of that place.

15. Jun 5 1821 (Tuesday)
Married at Baltimore on Sunday at 27th ult. by Rev. George Dashiell,
  Mr. John Wall to Miss Ann S. Ringgold.
Died on Saturday last Dr. John Metzgar, Sen. of Bottstown, in his 78th
  year.

16. Jun 26 1821 (Tuesday)
Married on Sunday last at Poplar Grove by Rev. Habbelstein, Dr. Luke
  Rouse of this borough to Miss Louisa Beitzel.
Died on Monday the 11th inst. in his 60th year, James Buchanan, Esq.,
  of Mercersburg.

17. Jul 3 1821 (Tuesday)
Married at Gettysburg on Tuesday evening the 19th ult. by Rev. John
  Herbst, William McClellan, Jr., Esq., to Miss Mary Hersh, dau. of
  John Hersh of that place.

Died suddenly on Saturday last in this borough, Mr. George F. Doll in
his 30th year.
- On Sunday last Mr. Michael Koons of this place.

18. Jul 24 1821 (Tuesday)
Married at Poplar Grove on Sunday 22nd inst. by Rev. Henry
Habliston, Charles Diehl, Jr., son of Jacob, to Miss Leah Luttman,
dau. of John Luttman, all of York township.
Died on Sunday morning last, Mr. Christopher Stoehr.
- On Monday morning last, George Haller, Esq of this borough.

19. Aug 6 1821 (Tuesday)
Married on Thursday week at Lewisberry Mr. Jacob Eppley to Miss
Jane McGrew.
- On Thursday evening last by Rev. Mr. Schmucker, Mr. Noah Dolb to
Miss Eliza Metzel, both of this borough.
Died last week at Lewisberry at an advanced age, Mrs. Mary Kaufman,
wife of John Kaufman, Sr. of that place.
- On Saturday last, Elisa Ann Ebert, infant dau. of the late Michael
Ebert of this borough.

20. Aug 28 1821 (Tuesday)
Died on Friday evening last in this borough, Mrs. Christina Spangler,
widow of Baltzer Spangler, in her 81st year.
-Suddenly on Wednesday last, Mrs. Freet, wife of Jacob Freet, miller.
- On Friday last, Mr. Thomas Ingles, of this borough.
- On Sunday evening, Miss Mary Bierman, dau. of Abraham Bierman of
this place.

21. Sep 4 1821 (Tuesday)
Died on Friday morning last in this borough at an advanced age, Mrs.
Catharine Fischer, widow of the late John Fischer, Esq.
- On Saturday last, Emily Beard, dau. of Michael Beard, in her 6th
year.
- Yesterday morning, Catharine Fisher, dau. of Dr. John Fisher, in her
7th year.
- On Wed last at Columbia, Mr. Philip Gossler, formerly a resident of
this place.
- On Saturday last in Lower Chanceford, Mr. James M'Full.
- On Sunday last in same township, Mr. Robert Cameron.

22. Sep 11 1821 (Tuesday)
Died in this borough on Thursday morning last, Mr. Henry Faust,
printer in his 20th year.
- On Sunday last Mrs. Gottwalt of Bottstown.
- On Mon, the 3d inst at Lewisberry (York County) Mr. Philip
Frankeberger of that place.
- On Sunday morning in Harrisburg, Mrs. Mary Smith, wife of Chester
Smith, formerly of this place.

23. Sep 18 1821 (Tuesday)
Died on Thursday evening last at York-Haven, Dr. Christopher
Stoddart, formerly of Georgetown, D.C., a recent graduate of Doctor
of Medicine from the University of Pennsylvania.
- On Tuesday morning last in Fairview township at an advanced age,
Mrs. Abigail Millard, relict of the late Samuel Millard.

24. Sep 25 1821 (Tuesday)
Died on Wednesday last near this borough, Mr. Jonas Spanglerd, in his
77th year.
- On Thursday last at New Holland, Mrs. Frie, mother of the late Capt.
John Frie who died by drowning some weeks ago.
- On the 2d of August at the town of America, Illinois, William S.
Findlay, Esq., attorney at law and eldest son of the late governor of
Pennsylvania, in his 27th year.
- On Thursday last at the seat of Peter Hoke in Harford County, Md.,
Mrs. Eliza Hoke, wife of Jacob Hoke and only dau. of Samuel
Spangler of this borough.

25. Oct 2 1821 (Tuesday)
Died on Friday morning last Messrs. Jesse and Abdiel Meyers, sons of
Mr. David Meyers of this borough. The former was in his 20th year
and the latter in his 13th year.
- On Thursday last Mrs. Elizabeth Ziegel, relict of the late Thomas
Ziegel of this borough.
- On Monday the 24th inst, Mrs. Baumgardner, wife of John
Baumgardner, at an advanced age.
- On Sunday last the Rev. Constantius Miller, Pastor of the Moravian
Congregation of this place.
- On Thursday morning last, in his 19th year, John Kirk, son of Isaac
Kirk, Esq., of Lewisberry.

- On Tuesday last near the same place, Miss Mary Drorbagh, eldest dau. of Michael Drorbagh.
- Yesterday morning near the same place, in her 21st year, Mrs. Harriet Wanbagh, wife of Capt. John Wanbagh and dau. of Nathan Potts.

26. Oct 9 1821 (Tuesday)
Married at Lancaster on Saturday evening, the 29th ult. by Rev. Clarkson, Frederick Eichelberger, Esq., of the State Senate, to Miss Catharine Baker, dau. of the late Frederick Baker, Esq.
Died in Lancaster on Monday morning, the lst inst. Mr. George Price, editor of the Free Press in his 29th year.
- In Philadelphia on Fri, the 28th ult. Mr. George Helmboldt, printer and editor of the Independent Balance in his 43rd year.
- At Marietta on Sunday morning, the 22d ult in the 43rd year of his age, the Rev. William Kerr.

27. Oct 16 1821 (Tuesday)
Married on Wed evening last by Rev. Schmucker, Mr. Charles Kurtz to Miss Juliana Eichelberger, both of this place.
- At Litchfield, Conn. on the 25th ult. by Rev. Camp, Walter S. Franklin, Esq., attorney at law of this borough to Miss Sarah Buel, dau. of Dr. William Buel of the former place.

28. Oct 30 1821 (Tuesday)
Married in this borough on Sunday evening, 21st inst. John Stroman, Esq., to Mrs Catharine Shramm of this place.
Died at York-Haven on the 23d inst., Mrs. Ann Connolly, consort of Mr. Henry Connolly of that place in her 19th year.

29. Nov 6 1821 (Tuesday)
Married on Thursday last by Rev. Kraber, Mr. John Kalkgresser to Miss Barbara Decker both of Codorus township.
Died on the 24th ult., Mr. Christian Rupp of this borough in his 54th year.
- Last Wednesday morning in West Manchester township, Mr. John Scott.
- Last Wednesday in Fairview township, Mrs. Elizabeth Miller, wife of Henry Miller, Jr.

30. Nov 13 1821 (Tuesday) Died last evening Mr. John Hay,
   merchant of this borough and 2nd son of Jacob Hay, Esq., in his 28th
   year.

31. Nov 20 1821 (Tuesday) Married on Thursday the 1st inst. at
   Williamsport, Pa., by the Rev. N. R. Snowden, Joseph B. Anthony,
   Esq., attorney at law, to Miss Catharine Graffius, dau. of Abraham
   Graffius, Esq., formerly of this borough.

32. Nov 27 1821 (Tuesday)
   Married at Hanover on Thursday evening last by Rev. J. H. Wiestling,
   Mr. Samuel Weiser to Miss Cassandra Heckert, both of this borough.
   - On Sunday evening last by Rev. Myers, Mr. James A. Jacobs to Miss
   Catharine King, all of this borough.

33. Dec 11 1821 (Tuesday)
   Died on Thursday last, Mr. George Luttman of this borough.
   Married on Tuesday last by Rev. Craver, Mr. Daniel Gross to Miss
   Susan Coleman, both of Dover township.
   - On Thursday last by the same, Mr. Jacob Hantz, of Dover, to Miss
   Lena Hershey of Heidleburg township.

34. Jan 1 1822 (Tuesday)
   Married on Tuesday last by Rev. Crever, Mr. Englehardt Melginger to
   Miss Mary Layman, both of Dover township.
   - On Thursday last by the same, Mr. Peter Staugh to Miss Elizabeth
   Gross, of Dover township.
   - On Thursday last by Rev. Lucky, Mr. Robert Kirkwood, of Harford
   County, Md., to Miss Elizabeth Thompson, of Hopewell, York County.

35. Jan 29 1822 (Tuesday)
   Married on Thursday afternoon last by Rev. Schmucker, Mr. George
   Eicheleberger to Miss Sarah Diehl, dau. of Nicholas Diehl of Spring
   Garden township.
   - On same evening by Rev. Craver, Mr. Joseph Strickland to Miss
   Magdalene Knaub, both of West Manchester township.

36. Feb 12 1822 (Tuesday)
   Died on Tues, the 5th inst, Peter Kline, of Hellam township in his 79th
   year.

- Lately in the city of Dublin, Ireland, Mr. Henry Cox, at an advanced age, having returned to Ireland after living in this county for a number of years.

37. Feb 19 1822 (Tuesday)
Died on Saturday last in her 70th year, Mrs. Jackson of this borough.
- On same day, Mrs. Wampler, consort of Joseph Wampler, of this place.
- Yesterday morning, Mr. Patrick Irwin of York township.

38. Feb 26 1822 (Tuesday)
Died in this borough on Sunday incoming last, Mr. William Barnise, in his 35th year.

39. Mar 12 1822 (Tuesday)
Died on Sunday afternoon last, Mrs. Catharine Doudel, consort of Jacob Doudel, Sr. and dau. of Peter Dickel, in her 54th year.

40. Mar 19 1822 (Tuesday) Married on Thursday last, at Columbia, by Rev. Boyer, Mr. John Miller to Miss Mary Kaufman, both of the city of Lancaster.

41. Mar 26 1822 (Tuesday)
Married on Sunday evening by Rev. Schmucker, Mr. Adam Miller to Miss Elizabeth Decker, dau. of Jacob Decker, all of this place.
- On same evening by Rev. Schaeffer, Mr. Henry Allbright to Miss Catherine Bupp, all of this borough.

42. Apr 16 1822 (Tuesday)
Married on Thursday, 4th inst. by Rev. J. H. Wiestling, Dr. Ezra P. Starr, of Dover, York County, to Miss Eveline Will, dau. of Jacob Will, dec'd., of Petersburg, (Littlestown) Adams County.
Died on the 11th inst. Mr. Jacob Billet, of Spring Garden township, in his 48th year.

43. Apr 23 1822 (Tuesday)
Married on Monday evening, the 15th last, in this borough by Rev. Schaeffer, Mr. Jacob Graeff to Miss Mara Garber, both of Lancaster.
- On Thursday last by Rev. Kreber, Mr. George Lieberknecht to Miss Abel, dau. of George Abel of Windsor township.

Died on Sunday the 14th inst. at Lewisberry, York County, Samuel
Grove, Sr. in his 75th year.
- On Wednesday last in this borough at an advanced age, Mrs Stewart,
widow of John Stewart, Esq., former representative in congress.
- On the same day, Mrs. Ahl, wife of Daniel Ahl, of this place.
- On Friday last in his 27th year, Mr. George Diehl, only son of Mr.
Nicholas Diehl, near this borough.

44. Apr 30 1822 (Tuesday) Married on Tues, the 16th inst., in
Lancaster County by Rev. Dahoff, Mr. Jones G. Evinger to Miss Eliza
Wirtz.

45. May 7 1822 (Tuesday) Died on Apr 30, Miss Elizabeth Fry, dau.
of Peter Fry of Windsor township in her 23rd year.

46. May 21 1822 (Tuesday) Married on Sunday evening last by Rev.
Vinton, Mr. Robert Life, of Fredericktown, Md., to Miss Catharine
Shue, of this place.

47. May 28 1822 (Tuesday)
Married by Rev. Henry Habliston on Thursday, 16th inst. Mr. Levi Day
to Miss Delila Downs both of Shrewsbury township.
- By the same on Thursday last, Mr. Joseph Leth, Jr. to Miss
Catharine, dau. of Simon Augustine, Esq., of Windsor township.
Died on Friday last Mr. Frederick Zoeger in his 39th year at Eib's
Landing.
- In this borough on Saturday last, Dr. Samuel Brooks.

48. Jun 4 1822 (Tuesday)
Married on the 27th ult. by Rev. Mayer, Mr. Peter Hoke, of Harford
County, Maryland, to Mrs. Catharine Wiemer, widow of the late
Andrew Wiemer, of West Manchester township.
- On the 28th ult. by Rev. Leffler, Mr. John Fahs, Jr. of Buttstown, to
Miss Susan Ilgenfritz, dau. of Samuel Ilgenfritz of this place.
- On the 30th by Rev. Geistweit, Mr. Samuel Kaufman to Miss Polly
Wagner, both of Hellam township.
- Same day by Rev. Mayer, Mr. William Streber to Miss Susan
Emmett, both of this place.
Died in this borough on the 1st inst. Mr. Jacob Buyer in his 24th year.

49. Jun 11 1822 (Tuesday) Married on Wednesday evening last by
Rev. Mayer, Mr. Charles Wilson to Miss Lydia Eichelberger, 2nd dau.
of the late John Eichelberger of this borough.

50. Jun 18 1822 (Tuesday)
Married on Tuesday week by Rev. Hableston, Mr. Henry Dom to Miss
Catharine Warner of Chanceford.
- On the 13th inst. by the same, Mr. John Low to Miss Margaret
Mathews, both of Shrewsbury.
- On Thursday the 6th inst. by Rev. Winebrenner, Mr. John Smith to
Miss Catharine Snyder, both of Allen township, Cumberland County.
- On the 13th inst. by Rev. Engle, Mr. Jacob Triver to Miss Mary
Strickler, dau. of Mr. Jacob Strickler of Spring Garden township.

51. Jul 2 1822 (Tuesday) Died on Saturday last at Hanover in this
county, in his 68th year, Mr. Adam Forney.

52. Jul 16 1822 (Tuesday) Married at Shrewsbury, York County, by
Rev. Habliston, Mr. Joseph Fidler, age 60, of said place to Miss
Catharine B. Bofaeng, age 40, of Columbia.

53. Jul 23 1822 (Tuesday)
Married at Shrewsbury Thursday last by Rev. Habliston, Mr. Edward
Evans, of Codorus Forge, to Miss Julianna Steruitt, of Hellam.
Died Friday morning last Mr. Samuel Rouse, son of Dr. John Rouse, in
his 21st year.
- On Friday last in York township, Mr. Jacob Bitner in his 22nd year.
- On Saturday afternoon last Mrs. Maria Catharine Weiser, consort of
Martin Weiser, in her 68 year.
- Yesterday morning in this borough, Mr. Peter Sears in his 30th year.

54. Jul 30 1822 (Tuesday)
Died on Saturday evening last near this borough Mrs. Ford (widow) at
an advanced age.
- On Sunday morning last, Mr. George Smith, son of Robert Smith of
this borough, in his 24th year.
- On Sunday in Newbury township, at a very advanced age, Mr.
Nathan Thomas.

55. Aug 6 1822 (Tuesday)
Married on Friday morning last by Rev. Stechman near this borough, Mr. Charles Lauman to Miss Sarah Schriver, both of this place.
- On Thurs, Aug 1st, at Shrewsbury by Rev. Habliston, Mr. Jacob Kaltreiter to Miss Sarah Shaeffer, of Shrewsbury township.
Died in this borough on Saturday morning last, Capt. Robert Ross, alias Jones.

56. Aug 20 1822 (Tuesday)
Married in this borough Thursday last by Rev. Vinton, Mr. Jesse Gratz to Mrs. Rebecca Machlin, both of Warrington township.
- On the 6th inst. by Rev. Geistweit, Mr. Samuel Ledber to Miss Lydia Heltze, both of Windsor.
Died on the 12th inst. in Strasbury township, Mrs. Catharine Miller, consort of Andrew Miller, in her 65th year.
- On the 14th in York township, Mrs. Morx, wife of Jacob Morx, at an advanced age.
- On the 9th inst. Christian Graeff of Paradise township in his 50th year.

57. Aug 27 1822 (Tuesday)
Married on Sunday last by Rev. Geistweit, Mr. Samuel Spangler, of Casper, to Miss Elizabeth Bowers, dau. of Jacob Bowers, Esq., of Adams County.
Died on the 4th inst. Mr. Jacob Tyson, in Windsor township.
- On the 20th inst. Mr. John Landis of same township.
- On same day in Hallam, Mr. George Dietz in his 62nd year.

58. Sep 3 1822 (Tuesday)
Died yesterday morning in Hanover, York County, Mr. David Myers, innkeeper.
- On Thursday evening last, Mrs. Sarah Hart, wife of John Hart of Fairview Township.
- On Saturday last, Samuel Garretson of Newbury Township at an advanced age.

59. Sep 10 1822 (Tuesday)
Married on Sun, the 1st inst., at Hanover by Rev. Melsheiner, Mr. Peter Johnson, of Baltimore, to Miss Wilhelmina Reigart, of the former place.

- On Thursday last at Gettysburg, Mr. Michael R. Clarkson to Miss Louisa Harper, dau. of the late Robert Harper, both of that place.

60. Sep 24 1822 (Tuesday) Died on Saturday evening last and in his 37th year, Mr. Frederick Bentz, Jr., only son of Mr. F. Bentz of this borough.

61. Oct 1 1822 (Tuesday)
Married on Wednesday evening last at Philadelphia by Rev. Van Vleck, Mr. Philip A. Small, merchant of the house of Geo. Small & Son, of this borough, to Miss Sarah Lattimer, dau. of the late William Lattimer, Esq., of Philadelphia.
- On Thursday evening last in this borough by Rev. Rahauser, Mr. William Wagner to Miss Margaret Spangler, dau. of the late Daniel Spangler, Esq., both of this place.
- On Sunday last at Maytown, Lancaster Co., Mr. Rudolph Miller of this borough to Miss Lydia Stoner of the former place.
- On same day at Hanover by Rev. McIsheimer, Dr. Francis Koon of this borough to Miss Elizabeth Hiestand, dau. of Abraham Hiestand of Spring Garden township.
- On Wednesday evening, 18th ult. at Philadelphia by Right Rev. Bishop White, Mr. James Coleman, Esq., son of Robert Coleman of Lancaster, to Miss Harriet Dawson of Philadelphia.
Died on Thursday last in Windsor township at an advanced age, Mr. Adam Shenberger.
- On 15th ult. at Washington city, the Rev. Samuel Davis, minister of the Methodist Episcopal Church, in his 28th year.
- In Chilicothe on the 1st ult. Mr. Archibald M'Clean in his 41st year.
- On the 19th ult. Mr. William Sturgeon of Oxford.

62. Oct 8 1822 (Tuesday) Married on Tuesday morning last by Rev. Schmucker, Mr. Christian Stavely to Miss Catharine Bitner, dau. of Adam Bitner, both of York township.

63. Oct 15 1822 (Tuesday) Died in Pottstown on Thursday last, Mr. Peter List in his 57th year.

64. Oct 22 1822 (Tuesday)
Married in this borough on Thursday last by Rev. Leffler, Mr. Samuel Brooks to Miss Margaret Forster.

- On Sunday evening by Rev. Mayer, Mr. William Jordan to Miss Barbara Stoehr all of this borough.
- At Hanover same day Mr. John Odenwalt to Miss Julia Hay, dau. of Mr. George Hay of this borough.

Died in Lewistown, Mifflin County, on Monday, the 14th inst. Jacob Doudel, Jr. of this borough in his 30th year.

- On Wednesday morning in this borough Mr. Charles Smith, son of Mr. Robert Smith, in his 23rd year.
- At Boston on the 13th inst. Mr. Thomas M. Willing, Esq., of Philadelphia.
- In Arkansas territory, Col. Matthew Lyon, a revolutionary officer and member of Congress for many years.

65. Nov 5 1822 (Tuesday)
Married on Thursday last by Rev. Schmucker, Mr. Christian Raufenberger to Miss Catherine Miller, both of Shrewsbury township.
- On same day by the same, Mr. Joseph Funk to Miss Susan Rudy all of this place.

Died on Sunday morning last Mr. Martin Wieser, Sr. of this borough in his 72nd year.

66. Nov 12 1822 (Tuesday) Died at York Haven in this county Saturday morning last, Mr. Lewis Delamare in his 43rd year.

67. Nov 26 1822 (Tuesday) Died in Long Hollow, Huntingdon County on Saturday the 16th inst. Mr. John Iawin formerly of this place.

68. Dec 3 1822 (Tuesday) Married on Thursday the 21st ult. at Williamsport, Pa., by Rev. Bryson, Ellis Lewis, Esq., attorney at law, to Miss Josephine Wallace, both of that borough.

69. Dec 10 1822 (Tuesday) Married on Wednesday evening last near Shrewsbury by Rev. Habliston, Mr. Ovid Hard to Miss Elizabeth Winks, both of Baltimore County.

70. Dec 17 1822 (Tuesday)
Died on Monday the 8th inst. in Newbury township, Mrs. Elizabeth Arthur in her 41st year.
- On Thursday last in same township, Mr. Andrew Fortenbough, Sr. at an advanced age.

- In Fairview township on Tuesday last, Mrs. Elizabeth Bailets, wife of William Bailets and
- On Thursday last, William Bailets.

71. Dec 31 1822 (Tuesday)
Married on Wednesday evening last by Rev. Leffler, Mr. William Eatey, stage driver, to Miss Prudence Kendrick of York township.
- On the same evening by Rev. Moyer, Mr. Michael Geesy to Miss Catharine Minich, dau. of Capt. Jonathan Minich of York township.
- On Sunday evening last by Rev. Leffler, Mr. Michael Shue to Miss Eliza Waltemeyer, all of this borough.
Died on Wednesday last in Warrington township, Mr. Peter Stickel, in his 65th year.
- On Sunday morning last, Mr. John Dritt, son of the late Gen. Jacob Dritt, of Windsor township.
- In this city on Saturday the 14th inst. Mrs. Catharine Reynolds, mother to the editor of the Lancaster Journal, in her 70th year.
- On Friday evening the 20th inst in Columbia, Mrs. Harriet Jeffries, wife of Joseph Jeffries and dau. of Mr. Jacob Duchman, of Lancaster city.
- On Thursday morning 19th inst. at Warren in Chester County in his 23rd year, Mr. Henry Fahnestock, who formerly resided with Col. Mayer of Lancaster city.

72. Jan 7 1823 (Tuesday)
Married on Tuesday last by Rev. Mayer, Mr. Joseph Small to Miss Elizabeth Barnhart all of this borough.
- On same day by Rev. Habliston, Mr. Jacob Kramlin, of Windsor, to Miss Maria Streher, dau. of Adam Streher, of Hopewell.
- On same day by the same, Mr. Henry Hammond to Miss Sarah Coulston, both of Baltimore Co.
Died last week in Manchester township, in her 39th year, Mrs. Mary Wales, wife of William Wales.

73. Jan 21 1823 (Tuesday)
Married on Wednesday the 15th inst. at Hanover in this county by Rev. Melsheimer, Mr. George Young to Miss Susan Scholl, all of that place.

- On Thursday last at Harrisburg, Mr. John Morris, of Maryland, to Mrs. Margaret Gilchell, of New Cumberland. (This is her 5th marriage.)
Died in Lancaster on the 10th inst. Mr. William Dickson, printer and editor of the Lancaster Intelligencer.
- At Canandaigua, N. Y. on the 31st ult. Gideon Granger, Esq., late postmaster general and politician.
- In this borough on Saturday morning last, Miss Susan Luuman.

74. Jan 28 1823 (Tuesday)
Married in Lebanon County on Thursday week, Mr. John Cameron, of Harrisburg, to Miss Mary Schulze, sister of John Andrew Schulze, of Myerstown, Lebanon Co.
- On Wednesday evening last in this borough by Rev. Mayer, Mr. John Eichelberger, tanner, to Miss Emma Jones, youngest dau. of the late Robert Jones, all of this place.
- On Thursday evening last by the same, Mr. Borius Fahnestock, of Abbottstown, Adams Co., to Miss Sarah Wampler, of this borough.
- On same evening, Mr. Daniel Smith to Miss -- Michael, both of this place.

75. Feb 11 1823 (Tuesday)
Died on Thursday last, John Youse, Esq., of this borough in his 40th year.
- On Sunday morning last, Mr. Henry Kline, of Windsor township.
- On Sunday evening last, in Frey'stown, Mrs. Mary Erwin, wife of George Erwin and dau. of Peter Sprenkle, of York township.

76. Feb 18 1823 (Tuesday)
Married on Thursday evening last by Rev. Leffler, Mr. Jacob Stroman to Miss Elizabeth Comfort, all of this borough.
Died on Tuesday night last in the prime of life, Mr. Jacob Small, of Spring Garden township.

77. Mar 11 1823 (Tuesday)
Married on Sunday 2d inst. by Rev. Mayer, Mr. George King, of York township, to Miss Rachel Johnston, dau. of Mr. William Johnston, of Spring Garden township.
- On Thursday last by Rev. Schmucker, Mr. George Rudy to Miss Mary Earich, both of Hellam.

Died on Sunday morning last, Mr. Lawrence Kroan of Hellam
township.
- Yesterday morning, Mr. George Dietz, of Hellam township in his 94th
year. Mr. Dietz was one of the first settlers of that part of the
county.

78. Mar 18 1823 (Tuesday)
Married on Wednesday evening last by Rev. Muhlenberg, Washington
Hopkins, Esq., to Miss Mary Franklin, dau. of Hon. W. Franklin, all
of Lancaster city.
- At Lebanon on Monday morning the 3d inst. George W. Kline, Esq.,
to Miss Catharine Leinaweaver, dau. of Peter Leinaweaver, all of that
place.
- On Thursday last, near this place by Rev. Schmucker, Mr. Jacob Bott
to Miss Lydia Smyser, dau. of Mr. Michael Smyser of West
Manchester township.

79. Mar 25 1823 (Tuesday)
Married at Camden, Del., on the 6th inst. by Rev. Torbert, the Rev.
William Prettyman, of Baltimore, to Miss Eliza Barrett, of the former
place.
- On Tuesday evening last by Rev. Mayer, Mr. Nathan Worley, Jr. to
Miss Mary Long.
- On the same evening by Rev. Vinton, Mr. William Brown to Miss
Elizabeth Brenise, all of this borough.
- On same day by Rev. Stecher, Mr. John Reaman, of Shrewsbury
township, to Miss Elizabeth Rouse, dau. of Dr. John Rouse of this
borough.
- On Thursday last, near Lewisberry in this county, Mr. Andrew
Fortenbach to Miss Christiana Kauffman, only dau. of Jacob
Kauffman.

80. Apr 1 1823 (Tuesday)
Married on Tuesday last at Hanover, York County, by Rev.
Melsheimer, Mr. Henry Welsh to Miss Margaret Maria Small, dau. of
Peter Small, Esq., both of this borough.
- On Thursday evening last by Rev. Schmucker, Mr. Jacob Kotter, of
Shrewsbury township, to Miss Eliza Smyser, dau. of Mr. Jacob
Smyser, of West Manchester township.

Died on Thursday morning last in his 26th year Henry Miller, merchant, of this borough.

81. Apr 8 1823 (Tuesday)
Married on Tuesday last in Lancaster, Mr. Daniel Ahl to Miss Elizabeth Shaeffer, both of this borough.
Died on Wednesday evening last in Gettysburg, Col Alexander Cobean.
- On Saturday last, at an advanced age, Mr. Jacob Clingman, of Fry's town.
- On Sunday morning last, Mr. John Rosenbaum, of this borough in his 32nd year.

82. Apr 29 1823 (Tuesday)
Married yesterday by Rev. Schmucker, Mr. Thomas Lunnan to Miss Mary Hayes, both of this borough.
Died in this borough on the 23rd inst. in his 45th year, Mr. George Spangler, late of Philadelphia, wine merchant and youngest son of Baltzer Spangler, dec.

83. May 6 1823 (Tuesday) Died on Tuesday last in this borough in his 49th year, Mr. Peter Small.

84. May 13 1823 (Tuesday)
Married on Sunday evening last by Rev. Schmucker, Dr. Michael Hay, of Oxford, to Miss Margaret Worley, dau. of George Worley, of this borough.
Died on Tuesday last, Mr. Peter Bentz, of Conewago township in his 65th year.
- On Thursday week last, Mr. Jacob Sherman, youngest son of Gen. Conrad Sherman, late of Manheim township, York Co. in his 34th year.

89. May 27 1823 (Tuesday) Died on Friday evening last in this borough, Mr. Peter Spangler, son of late Rudolph Spangler, Esq., in his 38th year.

90. Jun 3 1823 (Tuesday) Died yesterday afternoon, in this borough, Mr. Frederick Kock, in his 33rd year.

91. Jun 10 1823 (Tuesday)
Married on Thursday last at Hanover, Mr. John Hiestand, of Spring Garden, to Miss Elizabeth Sulsbach, dau. of Mr. Henry Sulsbach of Hellam township.
- On Thursday evening last at Columbia by Rev. Boyer, Mr. William Boggs, merchant of Baltimore, to Miss Caroline Jeffries, of Columbia.
- On Thursday evening the 20th ult. at Carlisle, Mr. George Leas of Carlisle to Miss Mary Ann Steiner, of Frederick town, Md.
- On Wednesday last on Shelly's Island by Rev. Lochman, Mr. David Detweiler to Miss Susan Shelly, eldest dau. of Mr. John Shelly.
Died on Sunday the 1st inst. at Philadelphia, Mrs. Deborah M. Bowie, relict of Ralph Bowie, Esq., late of this place, in her 45th year.
- On Wednesday morning last, Mr. Joseph Todd, son of James Todd of Newbury township, in his 22d year.
- On Thursday last near this borough in his 81st year, Mr. Frederick Eichelberhger.
- On the 26th ult. in Manchester township, Mr. William Metzgar, in his 57th year.

92. Jun 17 1823 (Tuesday)
Died on Friday morning last in this borough, William Hay, infant son of the late Mr. John Hay.
- On Sunday morning last in this borough, Mr. David Cramer.
- On the 15th of May at Lewistown, John A. Shulze, infant of 6 months age.

93. Jul 1 1823 (Tuesday)
Married on Sunday last by Rev. Mayer, Mr. Andrew Newman to Mrs. Sarah Eichelberger, all of this place.
Died on Monday Jun 23 in her 23rd year, Mrs. Ann Criswell, wife of Robert Criswell of Peachbottom township.

94. Jul 22 1823 (Tuesday) Died at New Market, Va., on the 3d inst. in her 24th year, Mrs. Eleanora Schmucker, wife of Rev. Samuel Schmucker, formerly of this place.

95. Jul 29 1823 (Tuesday) Died At Landisburg, Perry Co., in her 78th year, Mrs. Sarah Miller, wife of Gen. Henry Miller formerly of this place.

96. Aug 19 1823 (Tuesday) Married on Thursday evening last in this borough, Mr. Eli Hendrix to Mrs. Rebecca Jacobs, widow of the late Capt. George Jacobs.

97. Sep 9 1823 (Tuesday)
Died on Wednesday last in Warrington township, Mrs. Jany Taylor, in her 79th year.
- On Friday last near this borough, Mr. Samuel Smith.
- On Sunday last in Hanover, Mr. John Stauter in the prime of life.

98. Sep 16 1823 (Tuesday) Died on Sunday the 31st of Aug last in Peachbottom township, Mr. James Patterson, in his 30th year.

99. Sep 30 1823 (Tuesday)
Died on Friday morning last in this borough, Mr. Reuben Harry in his 31st year.
- On Tuesday last at Pittsburg, Pa., Nathan Worley, Jr. son of Mr. Nathan Worley, of this place, in his 24th year.

100. Oct 21 1823 (Tuesday) Died in this borough on Sunday morning last, Mr. George Wagner in his 40th year.

101. Nov 11 1823 (Tuesday)
Married on Thursday evening last by Rev. Mayer, Mr. Henry Small, Jr. to Miss Catharine Mosey, dau. of Mr. John Mosey, all of this borough.
- On the same evening by Rev. Mayer, Mr. John Worley to Mrs. Isabella Schully, both of this place.
- On Thursday week at Hanover by Rev. Wiestling, Dr. John Culbertson to Mrs. Elizabeth Chester, all of that place.

102. Nov 18 1823 (Tuesday) Married on Thursday evening last at Hanover by Rev. Melsheimer, David Shultz, Esq., to Miss Elizabeth Forney, only dau. of Samuel Forney, all of that place.

103. Nov 25 1823 (Tuesday) Married on Thursday evening last by Rev. Schmucker, Samuel Barnitz, Esq., attorney at law, to Miss Sarah Demuth, dau. of Mr. John Demuth, all of this place.

104. Dec 16 1823 (Tuesday) Married at Friends meeting in this place on Fifth day last, Dr. Obadiah Dingee, of Lancaster County, to Hannah Welsh, youngest dau. of the late William Welsh of this borough.

105. Jan 13 1824 (Tuesday) Married on Thursday last by Rev. Craber, Mr. John Craber to Miss Eliza Doll, all of this place.

106. Feb 17 1824 (Tuesday)
Married on Thursday last by Rev. Schmucker, Mr. Jacob Wildie to Miss Elizabeth Forry, dau. of Rudolph Forry, of this borough.
Died on Friday morning last in this borough, Miss Elizabeth Billmeyer in her 68th year.
- On Wednesday morning last Elizabeth Spangler, dau. of Peter Spangler, late of this borough, at 13 months of age.
- In this borough on Saturday morning last Elizabeth Dritt, dau. of John Dritt, late of Windsor township, at 11 months of age.

107. Mar 2 1824 (Tuesday) Married on Thursday last at Harrisburg by Rev. Dr. Lochman, Mr. John Weitzel to Miss Nancy Fisher, dau. of David Fisher, both of Fairview township, York Co.

108. Mar 9 1824 (Tuesday)
Married on Thursday evening last by Rev. Schmucker, Mr. Daniel P. Weiser to Miss Catherine Jameson, dau. of Dr. Thomas Jameson, all of this borough.
- On Wednesday evening last by Rev. Leffler, Mr. Charles Laumaster to Miss Eliza Snyder, all of this borough.

109. Mar 16 1824 (Tuesday)
Married on Thursday last by Rev. Habliston, Mr. George Henry to Miss Catherine Zeigler, dau. of John Zeigler, innkeeper, all of Hopewell township.
Died on Saturday evening last, Miss Esamiah Kelly, dau. of Col. John Kelly of this co.
- On Wednesday last in West Manchester township, Mrs. Sprenkle in her 92nd year.
- On Thursday last in Manchester township, Mr. Daniel Diehl in his 46th year.

- At Easton, Pa., on Monday evening the 1st of March, Mr. Henry A. Hutter, one of the proprietors of "Easton Centinel," in his 24th year.

110. Mar 23 1824 (Tuesday)
Married on Sunday evening last by Rev. Leffler, Mr. William Laub to Miss Catharine Snyder, all of this borough.
- At Philadelphia on Tuesday evening by Rev. Wilson, D. D., Charles B. Penrose, Esq., of Carlisle, Pa., to Miss Valeria F. Biddle, dau. of the late Wm. M. Biddle, Esq., of that city.
Died in this borough on Friday last, Mr. Michael Beard.
- On Thursday last in this borough, Abigail Worley, widow of late James Worley in her 78th year.
- In Lausanne, Prince Hohenlohe in his 81st year.

111. Apr 6 1824 (Tuesday)
Married on the 4th ult., Capt. John Wanbauch to Mrs. Elizabeth Forbes, both of Newbury township.
- On Tuesday last at Littlestown, Mr. Daniel Barnitz, Jr. to Miss Susan Forney, dau. of late Adam Forney, both of Hanover.
- On Sunday last in this borough, Capt. Joseph W. Schmidt to Miss Knab, dau. of late Casper Knab, both of Manchester township.

112. Apr 13 1824 (Tuesday)
Married at Lewisberry, York County on Tuesday last by Rev. Helffenstein Jr., Mr. John Shelly of Dauphin County to Miss Lydia Herman of Lewisberry.
- On Saturday the 3d of April inst. John Smith, Esq., by Mr. Abner Parson to Miss Susan Muntis, dau. of George Muntis, both of Hopewell township.
Died on Monday morning last in this borough, Major General Henry Miller, distinguished officer of the Revolution and late Prothonotary of Perry County in his 72d year.

113. Apr 20 1824 (Tuesday)
Married on Thursday evening last by Rev. Mayer, Mr. Jacob Dietz to Miss Catharine Welsh, dau. of Mr. John Welsh, all of this place.
Died on Tuesday last in this borough Mrs. Julianna Carter, wife of B. Carter, in her 34th year.
- On the same day Mrs. Margaret Gardner, widow of the late Martin Gardner, in her 74th year.

- On Thursday last, Mr. Martin Ziegler, in his 53th year.
_ On the same day, Mary Hommer, in her 38th year.

114. Apr 27 1824 (Tuesday)
Died on Friday Apr 9th inst. Mrs. Agness Beaty, wife of William Beaty, of Peachbottom township in her 29th year.
- On Sunday last in this borough, Mr. Daniel Wampler in his 29th year.

115. May 11 1824 (Tuesday)
Married on Tuesday evening last by Rev. Schmucker, Mr. Daniel B. Weiser to Miss Matilda Pentz, dau. of Dr. John Pentz, all of this place.
- On Thursday evening at Baltimore, Mr. Christian Hildebrand Jr. of this place, to Miss Elizabeth Klinefelter, dau. of Michael Klinefelter, Esq., of that city.

116. Jun 1 1824 (Tuesday)
Died on Friday evening last David Cassat, Esq., attorney, in his 56th year.
- At Carlisle on Friday the 21st ult., Mr. George Phillips, editor of the Carlisle Herald, in his 45th year.
- At Baltimore on Monday the 24th of May last, General William H. Winder, in his 49th year.
- At Marietta, Ohio, on the lst inst. Gen. Rufus Putnam, in his 96th year.

117. Jun 8 1824 (Tuesday) Died on Wednesday morning last at Lewisberry in this county, Hannah Kirk, wife of Jacob Kirk, Sr., in her 41st year.

118. Jun 15 1824 (Tuesday) Died on Tuesday evening last, Andrew Ritter, Esq., in his 84th year.

119. Jun 22 1824 (Tuesday)
Died on Wednesday morning last Mrs. Maria Elizabeth Lenhart, relict of the late Godfrey Lenhart, Esq., of this borough in her 74th year.
- Near Hagerstown on Saturday afternoon last, David Cooke, Esq. formerly of Marietta, Pa., of which place he was the founder, in his 74th year.

120. Jun 29 1824 (Tuesday)
Died on Friday evening last, Mr. Christian Kreidler of this borough in his 69th year.
- On Friday the 11th inst. in Harford County, Md., Mrs. Amelia Harlan, consort of Joseph Harlan, Esq.

121. Jul 6 1824 (Tuesday)
Married on Tuesday last by Rev. Schmucker, Mr. Michael Snyser to Miss Eliza Lanius, dau. of Christian Lanius, Esq., all of this borough.
Died yesterday, Mrs. Mary Rogers, wife of Abraham Rogers, of Frystown.

122. Jul 20 1824 (Tuesday)
Died in New Market, York Co., on Friday the 9th inst., William Culbertson, Esq.
Married on Sunday last by Rev. Leffler, Mr. John Nes to Miss Sarah Keiser, both of Shrewsbury township.
- On the same day by Rev. Leffler, Mr. John Schrock to Miss Lydia Innerst, both of Shrewsbury township.

123. Jul 27 1824 (Tuesday)
Died on Tuesday last in his 28th year, Mr. George Dunn, of this borough.
- On Wednesday morning, Mr. Henry Epley, of Buttstown in his 58th year.
- At Reading on the 11th inst. in his 34th year, the Rev. George Shenfelter, Pastor of the Roman Catholic Church in that borough.

124. Aug 3 1824 (Tuesday) Married on Friday the 23d ult. Mr. Jacob Kirk, Sr. to Miss Hannah Meredith, both of Lewisberry, York Co.

125. Aug 24 1824 (Tuesday)
Married at Carlisle on the 16th inst. by Rev. Williams, the Rev. John Thorne, formerly Rector of Episcopal churches of Carlisle and Huntington, to Miss Susan Hamilton, dau. of late Judge Hamilton.
- At Buenos Aires on Jun 2, John Eschenberg, Esq., of Germany, merchant, to Miss Eliza Rodney, 2nd dau. of the late Caesar A. Rodney, Esq.

Died in this borough on Thursday last and in her 70th year, Mrs. Luttman, widow of late George Luttman, Sr., formerly steward of the Poor House.
- On Monday evening last in Lower Merion township, Montgomery Co., Pa., Charles Thompson, Esq., Secretary of the Revolutionary Congress, in his 95th year.

126. Aug 31 1824 (Tuesday)
Died in this borough on Tuesday last in her 17th year, Pamela Hamersly, third dau. of Mr. Robert Hamersly near this place.
- On Wednesday Mrs. Margaret Yesler, relict of Henry Yesler, dec, in her 74th year.

127. Sep 14 1824 (Tuesday) Died on Sunday evening last in this borough in his 80th year, Mr. John Haller, late of Buttstown.

128. Sep 28 1824 (Tuesday) Married in this borough on Sunday evening last by Rev. Mayer, Mr. George Danner to Miss Cornelia Taylor, both of Lancaster city.

129. Oct 5 1824 (Tuesday) Married on Thursday evening last by Rev. Schmucker, Mr. Charles Surger to Miss Sarah Schlosser, both of the borough.

130. Oct 12 1824 (Tuesday) Married in this borough on Sunday evening last, Mr. John Beck to Miss Hannah Reichart, both of this county.

131. Oct 19 1824 (Tuesday)
Married in this borough on the 12th inst. by Penrose Robinson, Esq., Cyrus Cooper, of Chester Co, to Asenath Ann Cooper, of Lancaster Co.
Died on Sunday last in Spring-garden township in her 51st year, Mrs. Ann Hamaker, wife of Christian Hamaker.

132. Oct 26 1824 (Tuesday)
Married in Hanover on Thursday last by Rev. McIsheimer, Mr. Eli Lewis, of York, late Editor of "York Recorder," to Miss Rebecca Forney, of that place.

- In this borough on Wednesday last by Rev. Dr. Cathcart, Mr. Hosea Webster of Augusta, Georgia, to Miss Maria Buel, dau. of Dr. William Buel of Litchfield, Connecticut.
- On Tuesday last by Rev. Schmucker, Mr. Israel Gartner to Miss Ann Hahn, dau. of Mr. John Hahn all of this place.
- On Sunday the 15th inst., Mr. John Test to Miss Mary James of this place.
Died on Wednesday evening last, Mr. Jacob Graybill in his 75th year of this borough, drowned in "Upp's Spring."
- On Friday in Windsor Township, Mr. Christian Rathfong.

133. Nov 2 1824 (Tuesday)
Married on Thursday last by Rev. Mayer, Mr. David B. Prince to Miss Mary Anderson, dau. of late James Anderson, Esq., of this borough.
- On the same day by Rev. Schmucker, Mr. Israel Smyser of this place to Miss Matilda Ebert, dau. of Mr. Daniel Ebert of West-Manchester.
- On Sunday evening last in this borough, Mr. Michael Graybill to Miss Nancy King.
Died on Friday last in her 23rd year, Mrs. Smith, wife of Joseph Smith of West-Manchester.
- On Saturday last in her 53rd year, Mrs. Nancy Hiestand, wife of Abraham Hiestand of Spring garden.

134. Nov 9 1824 (Tuesday)
Married on Tuesday evening last by Rev. Leffler, Mr. James Duff to Miss Catherine Welsh, dau. of Mr. Michael Welsh, all of this place.
- On Sunday evening last by Rev. Williams, Mr. Daniel Sleeger, printer, to Miss Sarah Sedgewick, both of this borough.

135. Nov 23 1824 (Tuesday)
Married on the 13 ult. at Friends' Meeting, Sandy Springs, Md., Benjamin Hallowell, late of Westown H. School, to Margaret Farquhar of the above place.
Died on Wednesday morning last in his 17th year, Mr. Washington Spangler, eldest son of Mr. Samuel Spangler of this borough.

136. Nov 30 1824 (Tuesday)
Married at Lancaster on Thursday evening last by Rev. Clarkson, Mr. Joseph Jeffries of Columbia to Miss Hannah Thomas, of Carnarvon township, Lancaster Co.

137. Dec 7 1824 (Tuesday)
Married on Wednesday evening last, Mr. Benjamin Bowman to Miss
Catherine Laumaster, both of this place.

138. Dec 14 1824 (Tuesday) Died on the 9th inst. Mrs. Margaret
Kelly, wife of Col John Kelly of Chanceford township in her 64th
year.

139. Dec 28 1824 (Tuesday)
Married on Thursday evening last by Rev. Schmucker, Mr. John
Graham to Miss Leah Miller, both of this borough.
- At Milton, Pa., by Rev. Friem, the Rev. Samuel Gutelius, of
Northumberland Co. to Miss Anna Mary Small, of this borough.
Died on Wednesday last, Sarah Ann Rudy, dau. of Mr. Jacob Rudy of
this borough.

140. Jan 4 1825 (Tuesday)
Married on Thursday night last by Rev. Leffler, Mr. John Beck to Miss
Mary Fars, all of this borough.
- On the same evening by Rev. Schmucker, Mr. Jacob Schlosser to Miss
Maria Ilgenfritz, dau. of Mr. Jacob Ilgenfritz, both of this borough.
- In Harrisburg on Thursday last by Rev. Vinton, Mr. Joseph Wiley, of
this borough, to Miss Elizabeth Bretz, of the former place.
- On Friday Dec 24 by Rev. Duffield of Carlisle, Dr. Curtis of New
Holland, York Co. to Miss Sarah Brown, of North Middletown
township Cumberland Co.
- On Thursday last by Rev. Lochman, Mr. William Wanbaugh to Miss
Margaret Kosel, both of this county.
- In Gettysburg on Thursday evening last by Rev. M'Conaughy, John
Hersh, Jr., Esq., to Miss Nancy Edie, dau. of Mr. David Edie, both of
that place.
Died in this borough on Wednesday last in her 55th year, Mrs.
Catharine Barnitz, wife of George Barnitz, Esq.
- On Friday last in her 44th year, Mrs. Sarah Newman, wife of Mr.
Andres Newman, of this borough.

141. Jan 18 1825 (Tuesday) Died on the 8th inst. at Uniontown, Pa.,
Mrs. Elizabeth Shriver, wife of James Shriver, Esq.

142. Jan 25 1825 (Tuesday)
Married at Harrisburg on Thursday last by Rev. Lochman, Mr.
Christian Martin, of Cumberland Co., to Miss Mary Bruckhart, dau.
of Daniel Bruckhart, of York Co.
Died on Tuesday last, Mrs. Margaret Harry, wife of Stephen Harry,
late of this borough.
- On Friday evening last in her 30th year, Miss Sarah Laub.

143. Feb 1 1825 (Tuesday)
Married on Thursday morning last by Rev. Dr. Cathcart, Mr. John
Morrison to Miss Margaret Morrison, dau. of Michael Morrison of
Springgarden township.
- On the same day by the same, Mr. Samuel Smith, merchant, to Miss
Elizabeth Ross, dau. of the late Alexander Ross, of Warrington
township.

144. Feb 15 1825 (Tuesday) Died at Philadelphia on Saturday the
5th inst. in his 80th year, Rev. Dr. Helmuth.

145. Mar 8 1825 (Tuesday)
Married on Thursday evening last by Rev. Mayer, Mr. Joseph Buatt, of
New Orleans, to Miss Charlotte Wilt, dau. of V. Wilt of this borough.
- On Tuesday last by same, Mr. Thomas Elliot, of Baltimore, to Miss
Charlotte Danner, dau. of Mr. Martin Danner, of this borough.
- On 22nd Feb last by Mills Hays, Esq., Mr. Abraham Harman to Miss
Elizabeth Caull, both of Lewisberry, York Co.
- On the same day by Rev. Pearce, the Rev. Samuel Kennerly, of
Virginia, to Miss Elizabeth Lutz, of York Co.
- On Tuesday the 22d ult. by Rev. Pringle, Mr. Henry Logan, Jr. to
Miss Martha O'Hail, both of Monaghan township, York Co.

146. Mar 22 1825 (Tuesday)
Married on Thursday evening last by Rev. Leffler, Mr. Samuel
Mundorf to Miss Lucinda Fahs, both of this borough.
- On Sunday morning last by Rev. Davis, Mr. William Yocum to Miss
Alcinda Davis, both of this place.
Died on Wednesday last Mrs. Stroman, wife of Henry Stroman of this
borough.
- On Tuesday last, Col. Christopher Dosch of Windsor township.

147. Mar 29 1825 (Tuesday)
Married on the 17th ult. by Rev. Schmucker, Mr. Jacob Ginter to Miss
Margaret Furry, dau. of Rudolph Furry, both of this borough.
- On Thursday evening last by the same, Mr. Pennington Stoner to
Miss Elizabeth Haughman of this borough.
Died on the 19th inst. at Providence, Rhode Island, Miss Rhoda Mason
Richmond, dau. of William Richmond, Esq.

148. Apr 5 1825 (Tuesday)
Married on Thursday evening last by Rev. Leffler, Mr. Francis L.
Koons to Miss Lydia List, both of this borough.
- On the same day by Rev. Mayer, Mr. Gabriel Baer to Miss Charlotte
Spangler, dau. of Jesse Spangler, of this place.
- On Sunday morning last by the same, Mr. David Mayer to Miss
Catharine Wagner, both of Paradise township.

149. Apr 12 1825 (Tuesday)
Died on Friday morning last in his 38th year, Mr. Emanuel Spangler.
- On Saturday evening, Mr. Daniel Heckert in his 38th year.

150. Apr 19 1825 (Tuesday)
Died on Sunday morning last, Mrs. Catherine Dellow, of this borough
in her 73rd year.
- On Friday evening, Apr 1st, in Birmingham, Chester co in his 70th
year, Mr. Edward Darlington, former Representative of the State
Legislature.

151. May 10 1825 (Tuesday) Married on Tuesday evening last by
Rev. Schmucker, Mr. Jacob Eisenhart, of West Manchester township,
to Miss Eliza Schmucker, dau. of Rev. J. G. Schmucker, of this place.

152. May 24 1825 (Tuesday)
Married on Tuesday evening last by Rev. Schmucker, Dr. Samuel H.
Hugh, of Fawn township, York Co., to Miss Mary Ann Spangler, dau.
of George Spangler, Esq., of this borough.
- On Thursday the 12th inst. by Rev. Boyer, Mr. John Hoover to Miss
Catherine Gundacker, both of Lancaster Co.
- On Thursday last in this borough by Rev. Boyer, Mr. Nathaniel
Gillespy to Miss Rebecca Cooper, both of Columbia, Lancaster Co.

Died in this borough on Wednesday last in his 72d year, Mr. Abraham Miller.

- On Sunday morning last in this borough, Mr. Abraham Danner in his 41st year.

- On Apr 15th near Statesville, N. C., Mr. Henry Dillo, tanner, a native of Lancaster in his 50th year while traveling.

153. May 31 1825 (Tuesday) Died on Sunday the 15th inst., Mr. Eli Updegraph of Ligonier Valley, Westmoreland Co., in his 52nd year.

154. Jun 14 1825 (Tuesday)
Died in this borough on Saturday last, Mrs. Mary Test, wife of Mr. John Test, of this place.

- On Tuesday last near this place, Mr. George Michael Peter in his 75th year.

- On Friday the 10th inst. in York township, Mr. Lorentz Shultz, formerly of York in his 62nd year.

- At New Berlin, Union Co., on the 4th inst. Mrs. Mary Merrill, wife of James Merrill, Esq., of that place.

155. Jun 21 1825 (Tuesday)
Died in this borough on Tuesday evening last, Mr. Peter Rupp in his 38th year.

- On Wednesday evening last in this borough, Samuel Koons, son of John Koons (chairmaker) in his 7th year.

- In York township on Saturday morning last, Mrs. Catherine Sower, wife of Casper Sower.

- At Philadelphia on Sunday night, 12th inst. George Latimer, Esq., in his 75th year.

156. Jun 28 1825 (Tuesday)
Died in this borough on Thursday last, Mrs. Susan Jessop, wife of Jonathan Jessop.

- On Thursday night last, Mr. Casper Lehr, of East-Manchester township.

- At Reading on Saturday the 11th inst., Mrs. Elizabeth Hiester, consort of Gen. Joseph Hiester, late Gov. of Pa., in her 76th year.

157. Jul 5 1825 (Tuesday)
Married in this borough on Tuesday last by Rev. Cathcart, Mr. Peter
D. Barth to Miss Mary Clement.
- On Thursday evening last by Rev. Boyer, Mr. John Lansinger to Miss
Rebecca Neff, all of this place.
Died in this borough on Friday night last, Mr. Charles Goodyear in his
31st year.

158. Jul 12 1825 (Tuesday)
Died at his father's residence in Washington, Pa., on Wednesday
morning, 27 June, in his 23rd year, Mr. John Steen.
- On Saturday last in this borough at an advanced age, Mrs.
Houseman.
- On Saturday morning last in this borough, Elizabeth Shetter, dau. of
Mr. George Shetter in her 3rd year.

159. Jul 26 1825 (Tuesday)
Married on Thursday evening last by Rev. Schmucker, Mr. George P.
Kurtz to Miss Eliza Fisher, dau. of Dr. John Fisher of this borough.
Died on Tuesday last at Dover in this county in his 23rd year, Mr. Levi
Aughinbaugh, son of J. Aughinbaugh, Esq., of that place.
- In this borough on Friday last, Mr. William Shunk, Hatter, formerly
of Taneytown, Md.
- At London on 9 June in his 82nd year the Rev. Abraham Rees,
D.D.L.L.D. Editor of the Cyclopoedia.

160. Aug 2 1825 (Tuesday)
Married in this borough on Thursday last by Rev. Schmucker, Mr.
Henry Kochenour to Miss Catherine Hoffman, both of Conewago
township.
- On the same evening by the same, Mr. Daniel Waltman, of Hanover,
to Miss Elizabeth Gabriel, of this borough.
Died on Sunday morning last in her 48th year, Mrs. Catherine Barnitz,
with of John Barnitz, Esq., of this borough.
- On Sunday last in this borough, Mr. William Linton, of Upper Oxford,
near Cochransville, Chester Co., in his 32nd year.

161. Aug 9 1825 (Tuesday)
Married at Philadelphia on Thursday the 28th ult. by Rev. Heltenstein, the Rev. Augustus H. Loehman, of Harrisburg, to Miss Anna Maria Partenheimer, dau. of Mr. Adam Partenheimer, of Philadelphia.
Died at Hanover on Friday evening last, Charles Melsheimer, Esq., former Editor of "York Recorder" in his 46th year.

162. Aug 16 1825 (Tuesday)
Married in this borough on the 11th inst. by Rev. Schmucker, Dr. Henry Bowman, of Ephrata, to Miss Elisa H. Narr, of East Hempfield, Lancaster Co.
Died at Lancaster on Sunday morning last at an advanced age, Robert Coleman, Esq.
- At Cuba on 26 July in his 25th year, Mr. Henry Gottwalt, carpenter, formerly of this borough.

163. Aug 23 1825 (Tuesday) Died on Tuesday morning last in her 15th year, Miss Julia Ann King, dau. of Mr. Philip J. King, near this borough.

164. Sep 6 1825 (Tuesday) Died in this borough on Thursday last in her 36th year, Mrs. Boyer, consort of Rev. Stephen Boyer, of this place.

165. Sep 13 1825 (Tuesday) Married on Wednesday last by Rev. Boyer, Mr. James Lattmer , of the Island of St. Thomas, West Indies, to Miss Sarah Cathcart, dau. of Rev. Dr. Robert Cathcart of this borough.

166. Sep 20 1825 (Tuesday)
Married on Thursday evening last by Rev. Leffler, Mr. Jacob Upp, Jr. to Miss Ann Spangler, dau. of late Daniel Spangler, Esq., both of this borough.
Died in this borough on Wednesday evening last in his 21st year, Mr. William Michael, formerly of Hanover, York Co.

167. Oct 25 1825 (Tuesday)
Married on Thursday last by Rev. Schmucker, Mr. William Beard, of New York City, formerly of this place, to Miss Arah Hubley of this borough.

Died on Saturday the 9th inst. General John Edie of Gettysburg, Pa.,
in his 71st year.

168. Nov 1 1825 (Tuesday)
Married at Mount Airy, Shenandoah Co., Va., on Wednesday evening
the 12th ult. by Rev. Meyerheffer, the Rev. Samuel S. Schmucker, of
New Market, to Miss Mary Catherine Steenbergen, dau. of W.
Steenbergen, Esq.
Died on Saturday evening last, Mr. William Eichelberger of West
  Manchester township.
- On the 28th ult. Mrs. Eleanor McAllister, consort of James McAllister
of Hopewell in her 69th year.

170. Nov 8 1825 (Tuesday)
Married on Thursday last by Rev. Barry, Mr. William Vannard to Miss
Ann Russel, both of Manchester township.
- On Saturday the 29th ult. by Adam Wolf, Esq., Mr. James Beatty to
Miss Maria Stuart, all of New Holland.
Died on Tuesday last in his 76th year, Mr. John Dill, of Manchester
township.
- In Philadelphia on Tuesday evening last, Miss Sarah Hand Coleman,
youngest dau. of late Robert Coleman, Esq., in her 24th year.

171. Nov 22 1825 (Tuesday)
Died in this borough on Tuesday morning last, Mrs. Elizabeth Koons,
widow of late Francis Koons in her 85th year.
- On Saturday morning last, Mr. John Brown, a soldier of the
Revolution, in his 74th year.
- On the 5th inst in Conewago township, Mr. Jacob Meyer in his 73rd
year.
- On the 14 inst. in Middletown, Dauphin Co., Mr. John Croll in his
58th year, for many years an inhabitant of this borough.

172. Nov 29 1825 (Tuesday)
Married in Hanover on Thursday evening last, Mr. Henry Myers,
merchant of Hanover (formerly of this place) to Miss Catherine
Winebrenner of the same place.
Died on the 10th inst. on board the brig Edwin, Commodore
McDonough.

-In Philadelphia on Friday the 18th inst., Miss Caroline M. Henry, dau. of late Judge Henry of the city of Lancaster.

- On Tuesday the 22nd inst., Catharine Etter, wife of Samuel Etter, of York Co., in her 24th year.

173. Dec 6 1825 (Tuesday) Died at Lancaster on Friday morning last, Mr. Henry Reitzell in his 28th year.

174. Dec 27 1825 (Tuesday) Married on Thursday the 13th inst, Mr. Henry M. Connelly of York Haven to Miss Rachel Bugley of Harford Co., Md.

175. Jan 3 1826 (Tuesday)
Died Sunday afternoon the 25th ult. Rev. George B. Schaeffer, late rector of St. John's Church in this borough in his 28th year.
- On 13th inst. Christian Henutz Mayer in his 7th year.
- On the 15th inst. Louis Henry Mayer in his 15th year.
- On the 22th inst. Catherine Amelia Mayer in her 13th month and on the 25th inst. Virginia (?) Mayer, twin dau.
All children of Louis Mayer, Esq., of Philadelphia.
- On Sunday morning the 1st inst. Mrs. Elizabeth Koch, wife of Dr. Francis Koch of Hellam township.

176. Jan 10 1826 (Tuesday)
Died on Thursday evening last, Mr. William M'munn, in his 74th year.
- On Saturday last Jacob Gartner, son of Mr. Jacob Gartner in his 17th month.
- At Lancaster on Tuesday morning last in his 65th year, William Montgomery, Esq.

177. Feb 7 1826 (Tuesday)
Died on Saturday morning in her 38th year, Miss Elizabeth Huvner.
- On Sunday evening, Mrs. Catherine King, relict of Philip J. King, Sr. deceased, in her 77th year.
- Yesterday evening in this borough, Mr. Robert Grier.
- At Hamilton, Ohio about Jan 1st last, Mrs. Elizabeth Jones, relict of late Robert Jones of this place.

178. Feb 14 1826 (Tuesday)
Married on Thursday evening last by Rev. S. Boyer, Mr. John Truitt to
  Miss Sarah Heckery.
Died on Tuesday last in Buttstown in her 80th year, Mrs. Anna Myra
Smyser, widow of Col. Michael Smyser, dec'd.
- On the same day in this borough, Mr. Andrew Herman in his 32nd
year.
- On Friday last in Buttstown in her 60th year, Mrs. -- Lindt, widow of
Peter Lindt, dec'd.

179. Feb 21 1826 (Tuesday)
Married on Sunday week last by Rev. Tidings, Mr. John Hannewalt of
  Shrewsbury to Miss Hannah Gordon of Newholland.
- On Thursday last in Marietta Mr. John Martin to Miss Fanny
Buehler.
- On the same day Mr. John Stuart to Miss Sarah Burkhauser, both of
Codorus Forge, York Co.
Died on Tuesday last, Mrs. Anna Mary Spangler, consort of Mr.
  William Spangler, of this borough in her 32nd year.
- On the same day in her 22nd year, Mrs. Barbara Welsh, consort of
Charles Welsh, of this borough.
- On the 5th inst. in his 78th year, Mr. Jacob Felty, a soldier of the
Revolution.
- On the 22nd ult. Robert K. Lowry, Esq., formerly of York Springs,
Adams Co.

180. Mar 7 1826 (Tuesday)
Married on Thursday evening by Rev. Seifert, Mr. James Edwards to
  Mrs. Catharine M'Allen, all of New Holland.
Died on Saturday evening 25th ult. in her 80th year, Mrs. Margaret
  Dessenburgh, consort of late Anthony Dessenburgh of Manchester
  township.
- On Monday last Mr. John Cabute, of Manchester township.
- On Thursday last in her 13th year, Miss Magdalena Rudy, dau. of Mr.
George Rudy, of Manchester township.
- On Friday evening last, Miss Susan Miller dau. of John Miller.

181. Mar 14 1826 (Tuesday)
Married on Tuesday evening by Rev. Barry, John Voglesong, Esq., to
  Miss Isabella Penfield.

- On Thursday evening by Rev. Geistweit, Mr. George Welsh to Miss --
Wilt, dau. of Mr. Peter Wilt, all of this place.

182. Mar 21 1826 (Tuesday)
Married at Lewisberry, York Co., on Thursday last by James Todd,
Esq., Mr. David Herman to Miss Rebecca Lewis, dau. of Dr. Webster
Lewis, of the above place.
- At Hanover on Thursday last by Rev. McIsheimer, Mr. Charles
Stillinger, of this borough, to Miss Catharine Landt, dau. of Peter
Landt, dec'd. of West Manchester township.
Died last week Mrs. Elizabeth Wentz, consort of Mr. -- Wentz, of
Manchester township.
- On Wednesday last in his 45 year, Mr. Abraham Roth of Manchester
township.
- On Thursday last, George Finfrock, youngest son of Philip Finfrock of
Manchester township.

183. Mar 28 1826 (Tuesday)
Married on Thursday last by Rev. Schmucker, Mr. Jacob Kindig of
Liverpool, York Co. to Miss Mary Mosey, dau. of Mr. John Mosey of
this borough.
- On Thursday last by Rev. Kriber, Mr. John Krone to Miss Catherine
Sprenkle, both of Spring Garden township.
- On Sunday evening last by Rev. Geistweit, Mr. Charles Spangler, of
this borough to Miss Sarah Shultz, dau. of Peter Shultz of West
Manchester township.
- On Tuesday evening last, Mr. Adam Henry to Miss Catharine
Gottwalt, both of this borough.
- At Lancaster on Thursday last by Rev. Endress, Mr. John Witmer of
Donegal township, Lancaster Co., to Miss Jane Fitz of Hellam
township, York Co.
Died on Friday last Emanuel H. Hantz, son of Jacob Hantz of this
borough in his 4th year.
- On Saturday last in this borough, Dr. John Pentz in his 48th year.

184. Apr 4 1826 (Tuesday)
Married on the 28th ult. by Rev. Myers, Mr. Jacob Becker to Miss
Marriet Schultz, both of York Co.
Died in this borough on Thursday last in her 45th year, Mrs. Catharine
Reese, consort of Mr. William Reese dec'd.

- On Sunday evening last, Mr. Michael Eurich.

185. Apr 11 1826 (Tuesday)
Married at Fredericktown, Md., on Tuesday the 28th ult. by Rev.
   Johns, Rev. William Armstrong to Miss Eliza Johnson, dau. of Major
   Roger Johnson.
Died at Washington City on the 30th ult. Mr. John H. Cotvin, former
   editor of Republican Advocate at Fredericktown in his 48th year.
- At Holgate, near York, England, on the 23rd Feb, Mr. Lindsey
   Murray, author of English Grammar in his 90th year, a native of
   Pennsylvania.

186. Apr 18 1826 (Tuesday)
Married on Tuesday evening last by Rev. Schmucker, Mr. Daniel
   Hettshu, of Lancaster, to Miss Mary Weiser, dau. of Mr. Samuel
   Weiser of this borough.
- On Tuesday the 28th ult by Rev. Williamson, Mr. Joseph Eppley of
   Newbury township, York Co., to Miss Polly McCann, dau. of Mr.
   Peter McCann, of Lisbarn, Cumberland Co.
Died on 2nd Apr inst. in Beaver co, Pa., Mr. James Miller, formerly of
   Fayette co, son of late Mr. Robert Miller of Neal's Hole, Chanceford
   township in this county.
- On Saturday last in this borough, Mrs. -- Norris, wife of Mr. William
   Norris.

187. Apr 25 1826 (Tuesday)
Died on Saturday last, Mrs. Susan Weiser, consort of Mr. Samuel
   Weiser, Hatter) of this borough in her 32nd year.
- On Saturday 15th April at the residence of her son-in-law, Thomas
   Smith, Esq., near Darby, Mrs. Jane Henry, relict of the late
   Honorable Joseph Henry, Esq., of Lancaster.
- On Monday last in Frystown, Mr. Sharbone, in his 84th year.

188. May 2 1826 (Tuesday)
Died on Thursday evening last, Mr. Andrew Barland.
- On Saturday evening in Windsor township at an advanced age, Mrs. --
   Dritt, widow of the late Gen Jacob Dritt.

189. May 9 1826 (Tuesday) Married on Thursday evening last by

Rev. Schmucker, Mr. Daniel Willhelm to Miss Louisa Frey, both of this borough.

190. May 30 1826 (Tuesday) Married on Thursday the 25th inst by Rev. Hail, Mr. Samuel Ramsay to Miss Catharine Wilson, both of Conewago township.

191. Jun 13 1826 (Tuesday) Married at Chambersburg, Pa., on the 11th ult. Mr. John Buckius, of Canton, Ohio, to Mrs. Zinn, of this borough.

192. Jun 20 1826 (Tuesday) Married at Columbia by Rev. H. B. Shaffner, Mr. Andrew Rutter to Miss Susanna Gibson, dau. of Mr. James Gibson, both of York Co.

193. Jun 27 1826 (Tuesday)
Married at Harrisburg on Tuesday evening last by Rev. Clemson, Dr. Francis Knoh of this borough to Miss Nancy Hiestand, dau. of Abraham Hiestand of Springgarden township.
- At Lancaster on the 15th inst Mr. Jacob Bahn to Miss Elizabeth Liebhart, dau. of Jacob Liebhart, Esq., all of Hellam township.
- On the 11th inst. by Rev. Douglass, Mr. Moses Kendall to Miss Mary McArthur, both of Wrightsville, York Co.
- On Thursday last by Rev. Leffler, Mr. Casper Sour of York township to Mrs. Maria Arnold, of Dillsburg.
- On the 18th inst. Mr. William Goodridge, of this borough, to Miss Evelina Wallace of Baltimore.
Died in this borough on Thursday morning last, Mrs. Mary Shire, consort of Mr. David Shire.

194. Jul 4 1826 (Tuesday) Married in this borough on Tuesday last by Rev. Bayer, Mr. Christian Miller, Jr. of Marietta, to Miss Mary Guy, dau. of Mr. John Guy of Donegal township, Lancaster Co.

195. Jul 11 1826 (Tuesday) Died at Lancaster on the 2nd inst. Colin Cooke, Esq., in her 32nd year.

196. Jul 18 1826 (Tuesday)
Married on Sunday last by Rev. Barry, Mr. Daniel Jackson, of York Haven, to Mrs. Delia Jefferson, of this borough.

Died at Harrisburg on the 10th inst. Rev. George Lochman, pastor of the Lutheran Church of that place, in his 53rd year.

197. Aug 8 1826 (Tuesday)
Married on Sunday evening last by Rev. Geistweit, Mr. George Ziegler, to Miss Sally Manx, both of Springgarden township.
Died in this borough yesterday morning, Mr. Robert McMunn in his 21st year.
- On Tuesday morning last in his 40th year, Mr. Henry Hay, merchant of this borough.

198. Aug 15 1826 (Tuesday)
Married in this borough on Thursday evening last by Rev. Leffler, Mr. Jonas Meyers, of Lititz, Lancaster Co., to Miss Sarah Hidebrand, dau. of Mr. Christian Hidebrand, Sr. of this borough.
Died on Wednesday morning last in this borough, George Washington Ahl, son of Mr. Daniel Ahl, in his 10th month.
- On Friday last, Elizabeth Boyer, dau. of Mr. Henry Boyer, of this borough in her 17th month.

199. Aug 22 1826 (Tuesday)
Married at Marietta on the 10th inst. by Rev. Douglass, W. C. Carter, Esq., formerly of this borough to Mrs. Anne Smith of the former place.
Died at Lancaster on Thursday afternoon, John Reitzel, Esq., in his 70th year.

200. Aug 29 1826 (Tuesday)
Died in this borough on Saturday last, Mrs. Catharine Christiana Hildebrand, wife of Mr. Christian Hildebrand, Sr. in her 50th year.

201. Sep 12 1826 (Tuesday)
Married on Tuesday evening last by Rev. Geistweit, Mr. Charles F. Hoffmeier, merchant of Ephrata, Lancaster Co. to Miss Margaret Weiser, dau. of Samuel Weister, Esq., of this borough.
Died at Philadelphia on the 28th ult, Mrs. A. Wilson, relict of Rev. Joshiah Wilson of Chanceford, dec'd in her 48th year.

202. Sep 19 1826 (Tuesday)
Married at Frederick, Md., on Tuesday last by Rev. Schaeffer, Mr.
William Small, formerly of this place to Miss Maria Turbutt, dau. of
Capt. Nicholas Turbutt of that city.
Died at his residence in Wrightsville on Monday morning, the 11th inst.
James Speer, M.D.formerly of Gettysburg.

203. Oct 3 1826 (Tuesday)
Married on Thursday the 21st ult. by Rev. Melsheimer, Dr. George W.
Hinkle to Miss Deliah Wirt, dau. of Mr. Christian Wirt, both of
Hanover.
- On Thursday evening last by R. Hamersly, Esq., Mr. Adam Strouse,
of Roseville, to Miss Rebecca Morthland of Washington township.
Died on Tuesday last in his 30th year, Mr. Peter Feiser of York
township.

204. Oct 17 1826 (Tuesday)
Married on Thursday evening last by Rev. Schmucker, the Hon.
George Barnitz, Associate Judge of Court of Common Pleas of York
Co, to Miss Elizabeth Beitzell, both of this borough.

205. Oct 24 1826 (Tuesday)
Married on Sunday evening the 15th inst. at Lewisberry by Isaac Kirk,
Esq., Mr. William Nichols, merchant, to Miss Matilda Maxwell, all of
the above place.
Died at Fredericktown, Md., on Friday the 13 inst., Miss Mary Sharp,
formerly of this borough.
- On the 21st inst. Mrs. Margaret Dobbins, in her 37th year.

206. Nov 14 1826 (Tuesday)
Married on Friday the 3rd inst. by H. Hamersly, Esq., Mr. George
M'Millen, of Warrington, to Mrs. Jane Meyers, of Washington
township, York Co.
- At Northumberland on Thursday the 19th ult by Rev. Hood, James
Merrill, Esq., of New Berlin, Union Co. and formerly of this borough,
to Mrs. Sarah Hepburn, dau. of John Cowden, Esq., of the former
place.
Died on Saturday last in this borough, Mr. Baltzer Spangler in his 30th
year.

- On Friday night last in Windsor township, Mr. George Mengst in his 25th year.

207. Nov 21 1826 (Tuesday)
Married on Tuesday evening last by Rev. Geistweit, Mr. John Brenise to Miss Lydia Doll, both of this borough.
- On Wednesday last at Friends' Meeting, Phineas Davis, of this borough, to Hannah Taylor of West Manchester township.
- On the same day, Mr. W. Bentz Dehoff, of Dillsburg, to Miss Lynch, of Cumberland Co.
- On Thursday by Rev. Boyer, Mr. Thomas Cox to Miss Jane Baxter.
- On Tuesday last by Rev. Leffler, Mr. John Shank to Miss Mary Buser, dau. of Mr. Jacob Buser of this borough.

208. Dec 5 1826 (Tuesday) Died on Thursday last, Caroline Louisa Hildebrand, infant dau. of Mr. Christian Hildebrand, Jr.

209. Dec 12 1826 (Tuesday)
Died at Dunnianway in County Cork, Ireland, on 20th Sep last, Mr. Joshua H. Cox formerly of this borough.
- On Saturday last, Mr. John Myers of Freystown.

210. Dec 19 1826 (Tuesday) Married at Reading on Thursday last by Rev. Grier, Mr. Davenport Orrick, of Martinsburg, Va. (formerly of this place), to Miss Sarah M'Knight, dau. of John M'Knight, Esq., of Reading.

211. Jan 2 1827 (Tuesday) Died on Tuesday morning last, Mrs. Eleanor Dill, of the vicinity of Dillsburg in this county.

212. Jan 16 1827 (Tuesday)
Married at Columbia by Rev. Boyer on Tuesday the 2nd inst., Mr. Charles N. Wright to Miss Susan Stump, both of that place.
Died on Monday the 8th inst. in Springgarden township, Jacob Lefevre, Esq., in his 74th year.
- On Friday morning last in this borough, Mr. William Peters in his 36th year.
- On the 26th ult. in Baltimore, Nicholas W. Taylor, youngest son of Thomas Taylor of this borough.

-On Wednesday last at Chesnut Hill, Mr. William Schlatter, late of Philadelphia, merchant in his 43rd year.

213. Jan 23 1827 (Tuesday) Died at Philadelphia on Thursday morning in her 78th year, Mrs. Mary Morris, relict of the late Robert Morris, Esq., and sister of Bishop Whitt.

214. Jan 30 1827 (Tuesday) Married in this borough on Thursday evening last by Rev. Barry, Mr. Adam Axe to Miss Jane McKenzie, formerly of Alexandria, D. C.

215. Feb 20 1827 (Tuesday) Married at Harrisburg on Wednesday the 7th inst. by Rev. Herbst, Andrew G. Miller, Esq., to Miss Caroline E. Kurtz, dau. of Benjamin Kurtz, Esq., of that place.

216. Mar 6 1827 (Tuesday)
Married on Tuesday evening last by Rev. Schmucker, Mr. Bernard
 Beha to Miss Magdalena Nellinger, both of this borough.
- On Sunday evening last by Rev. Leffler, Mr. Emanuel H. Schroeder
 to Miss Leah Minnich, dau. of the late Simon Minnich dec'd., both of
 this borough.
Died on Thursday last in this borough, Mr. John Bailor in his 68th
 year.
- On Saturday afternoon in his 21st year, Mr. George W. Spangler,
 youngest son of late Daniel Spangler, Esq., dec'd.

217. Mar 13 1827 (Tuesday)
Married on Thursday morning last by Rev. Schmucker, Dr. George
 Sharer of Dillsburg, York Co., to Miss Eliza Eichelberger, dau. of Mr.
 Jacob Eichelberger of this borough.
- On Saturday the 3rd inst., Mr. Ephraim Walls to Miss Catharine
 Kerr, both of this place.
- On Sunday the 4th inst. by Rev. Teistweit, Mr. Charles Welsh to Miss
 Eliza Laumaster, both of this place.

218. Mar 20 1827 (Tuesday)
Died in this borough on Thursday morning last, Mrs. Charlotte Danner,
 wife of Abraham Danner, Sr. in her 72nd year.

- On Fri, Mr. John Brickle, a member of the York Volunteers which marched to Baltimore in 1814 and engaged in the battle of North Point.
- On Sunday night, Mr. Jacob Minnich.

219. Mar 27 1827 (Tuesday) Married on Thursday evening last by Rev. Schmucker, Mr. Samuel Ilgenfritz (blacksmith) to Miss Lydia Imfelt, both of this borough.

220. Apr 3 1827 (Tuesday)
Married on Thursday last by Rev. Cathcart, Mr. Mathew Grove to Miss Mary Gemmill, dau. of Robert Gemmill, Esq., of Chanceford township, York Co.
Died on the 26th ult. in his 12th year, Samuel Wagner, son of Mr. John Wagner, of this borough.

221. Apr 10 1827 (Tuesday)
Married on Thursday last by Rev. Schmucker, Mr. George Shulze, of Buttstown, to Miss Mary Michael of this borough.
- On the same evening by the same, Mr. George P. Ziegler to Miss Lenah Ilgenfritz, dau. of Mr. Samuel Ilgenfritz of this borough.
- On the same evening by the same, Mr. Jacob Wilt to Miss Elizabeth Frey of Manchester township.
- On the same evening by the same, mr. Samuel Metzgar to Miss Mary Frey of Manchester township.
Died on Saturday last in her 75th year, Hannah Welsh, relict of William Welsh, late of this borough, dec'd.
- On Thursday night the 29th inst. Dr. Henry Young of Shrewsbury township in his 55th year.
- On the 29th inst. Mr. Baltzer Faust of Shrewsbury township in his 34th year.
- At Hanover on Saturday morning, 31st inst. Mr. Paul Metzger, in his 84th year.

222. May 1 1827 (Tuesday) Married in Hopewell township on Thursday evening last by John Smith, Esq., Mr. Francis Worley to Miss Eliza Corben formerly of York.

223. May 8 1827 (Tuesday)
Married on Thursday last in Hopewell township by Rev. Cathcart, Rev.
  Stephen Boyer, of this borough, to Miss Mary Turner, dau. of the late
  Major Alexander Turner of Chanceford.
Died in Philadelphia on Sunday Apr 29th the Honorable William
  Tilghman, Chief Justice of Pennsylvania, in his 71st year.

224. May 15 1827 (Tuesday)
Married on the 3rd inst. by Rev. Vondersloth, Mr. Rudolph Spangler, of
  Paradise township to Miss Sarah Herbaugh, dau. of Jacob Herbaugh,
  of West Manchester township.
Died yesterday in this borough, Mr. John Kaufman.
- On Monday the 7th inst. Jacob Nell, in his 49th year, a member of
  the York Volunteer in 1814 and severely wounded at North Point
  battle.

225. May 22 1827 (Tuesday)
Married on Thursday last by Rev. Reily, Mr. George Overdorff to Miss
  Elizabeth Lenhart, both of Lancaster Co.
- On Sunday evening last by Rev. Hemphill, Mr. Peter Free of
  Manchester township to Miss Maria Dick of Freystown.

226. May 29 1827 (Tuesday)
Married in this borough Thursday evening last by Rev. Geistweit, Mr.
  John Ellby to Miss Cordelia Roman, both of Wrightsville, York Co.
- On the 24th inst. by Rev. Williamson, Mr. John Cresler of Carlisle to
  Miss Mary Jones, of Dillsburg, York Co.
- On Thursday last, Mr. -- Nicholson, of Emmittsburg, to Miss Ruth
  M'Guire, of Dillsburg, York Co.
- On the 24th inst. by James Alricks, Esq., Mr. John Summy to Miss
  Susanna Freeman, both of York Co.
Died on Monday 21st inst., Hannah Schlosser, dau. of Mr. John
  Schlosser of this borough in her 10th year.
- On Wednesday last in this borough, Mrs. Chistiana Karber, relict of
  George Karber, dec'd., in her 95th year.
- On Friday afternoon, a son of Mr. David Klinedienst of this borough,
  about 10 years of age, drowned while bathing in Codorus.

227. Jun 5 1827 (Tuesday)
Married on Tuesday evening last by Rev. Leffler, Mr. John Fahnestock
to Miss Amelia Lanius, dau. of Mr. Christian Lanius, both of this
borough.
- On Thursday morning last by Rev. Schmucker, Mr. Frederick
Baugher, Jr. of Abbottstown, to Miss Julia Upp, dau. of Mr. George
Upp of this borough.

228. Jun 12 1827 (Tuesday) Died in this borough on Friday evening
last, Mrs. Sarah Sanderson, consort of Mr. Samuel Sanderson.

229. Jun 26 1827 (Tuesday)
Married on Tuesday morning last Mr. Joseph Taylor, of Washington, to
Miss Juliet M. Hamersly, eldest dau. of R. Hamersly, Esq., of
Warrington township, York co and formerly of this borough.
Died on Saturday night in Springgarden township, Mr. John Rode, in
his 78th year.
- At Wheeling, on Monday the 11th inst. the Rev. John Armstrong,
former rector of St. John's Church of this borough in his 57th year.

230. Jul 24 1827 (Tuesday)
Married on Thursday evening the 19th inst. by Rev. Hall, Mr. Israel
Wolf to Miss Cassandra Shettley, both of this borough.
Died at Lancaster Saturday last, Mr. Mary Heitshue, wife of Daniel
Heitshue of that city and dau. of Mr. Samuel Weiser of this borough.

231. Jul 31 1827 (Tuesday)
Married on Wednesday morning last by Rev. Klugey, Mr. John Worley
to Mrs. Elizabeth Ebert, both of this borough.
Died on Wednesday last in this borough, Mrs. Margaret Ilgenfritz,
consort of Mr. Henry Ilgenfritz, in her 26th year.

232. Aug 7 1827 (Tuesday)
Married on Sunday evening last by Rev. Klugey, Mr. George Minnich
to Miss Ann Mary Buehyler, both of this borough.
Died at Philadelphia on Sunday morning the 29th ult. Miss Ann Greer,
dau. of late Robert Greer, Esq., dec'd. of this borough.
- Near Liverpool on the 2nd inst., Mrs. -- Kindig in her 17th year.
- On the same day, Ananias Miller, son of Christian Miller in his 17th
year.

- In this borough on 3rd inst. Mr. Lewis Keefer, in his 25th year.

233. Aug 21 1827 (Tuesday)
Married in this borough on Saturday morning the 18th inst. by Rev. Cathcart, Mr. David S. Barnum to Miss Sarah Gilmore, both of Baltimore.
- On Sunday evening the 19th inst. by Rev. Hall, Mr. John Stall to Mrs. Elizabeth Smith, both of this borough.
- At Lancaster on Saturday the 11th inst. by Rev. Endress, the Rev. Lewis Mayer, Prof of Divinity in the Theological Seminary of the German Reformed Church at Carlisle to Mrs. Maria Smith, of Lancaster.
Died on Wednesday morning last at Baltimore in his 17th year, Mr. Carvel Kelly, youngest son of the late James Kelly, Esq., of this place.
- In Wellsborough, Tioga Co. Pa., on Saturday the 11th inst. Elizabeth Lewis, dau. of Ellis Lewis, Esq., formerly of this county in her 3rd year.

234. Sep 4 1827 (Tuesday) Died on last Saturday morning in her 74th year, Mrs. A. M. Lauks, consort of Jacob Lauks.

235. Sep 18 1827 (Tuesday)
Married in Berlin on Thursday last by Rev. Albert, Mr. Charles Heckert, formerly of this borough, to Miss Lydia Hoke, dau. of Mr. Frederick Hoke of Warrington township, York Co.
Died in Chanceford township on Tuesday the 11th inst. Mrs. Elizabeth Douglass, in her 94th year.

236. Sep 25 1827 (Tuesday)
Married yesterday by Rev. Reily, Mr. Henry Gross to Miss Elizabeth Oberholtzer.
- By the same Mr. Jacob Dillinger to Miss Eve Klinefelter.
Died on Sunday morning in her 41st year, Mrs. Susanna Ziegler, wife of Peter Ziegler of Spring-garden township.
- On the 12th inst. at the residence of her mother in Harford Co., Md., Mrs. Rachael Connolly, wife of Mr. Henry Connolly of York Haven.

237. Oct 2 1827 (Tuesday)
Died on Sunday last in Spring Garden township, Mr. Adam Frey, eldest son of Mr. Jacob Frey in his 18th year.

- On the same day in Wrightsville, Mrs. Margaret Fahs, consort of Mr. Jacob Fahs formerly of this borough.

238. Oct 9 1827 (Tuesday)
Married on the 26th ult. in Philadelphia by Rev. Allen, Mr. Eli Kirk, formerly of this borough, to Miss Elizabeth Margaretta Palmer, youngest dau. of John B. Palmer, Esq., of that city.
Died in Wrightsville, on Thursday morning the 27th ult. in her 48th year, Mrs. Salome Shuff, consort of the late John Shuff formerly of Gettysburg.

239. Oct 16 1827 (Tuesday)
Married at Carlisle on Tuesday last by Rev. Keller, The Rev. Nicholas Sharrette to Miss Louise Spottswood, dau. of Capt. Lindsey Spottswood.
- In this borough on Thursday evening last by Rev. Schmucker, Mr. Benjamin Ziegler to Miss Maria Bentz, dau. of the late Dr. John Bentz.
- On the same evening by Rev. Hemphill, Mr. -- Hopkins to Miss Maria Jackson, both of this borough.

240. Oct 23 1827 (Tuesday)
Married on Thursday evening last Mr. Daniel Lehman to Miss Catharine Ehrman, both of this borough.
Died in Harrisburg on the 17th inst. the Hon. Jacob Bucher, Esq., Associate Judge in Dauphin Co. in his 64th year.

241. Oct 30 1827 (Tuesday)
Married on Thursday last by Rev. Schmucker, Mr. George Bentz to Miss Lydia Krone, both of this borough.
- At Hanover on the same day, Mr. John Small to Miss Eliza Rudisell, both of this borough.

242. Nov 6 1827 (Tuesday)   Married on Thursday evening last by Rev. Schmucker, the Rev. John G. Morris, pastor of 1st English Lutheran Church in Baltimore, to Miss Eliza Hay, dau. of Jacob Hay, Esq., of this borough.

243. Nov 20 1827 (Tuesday)
Married at Hanover on Thursday last, Mr. Samuel Weiser Jr. to Miss
  Ann Ilgenfritz, youngest dau. of Mr. Samuel Ilgenfritz, both of this
  borough.
- On the same day by Rev. Reily, Mr. Henry Scheffer to Miss Barbara
  Deisinger, both of Paradise township.

244. Nov 27 1827 (Tuesday) Died at Lancaster on Friday morning
the 16th inst. the Hon. Thomas Duncan, one of the Judges of the
Supreme Court of Pa.

245. Dec 4 1827 (Tuesday) Died on Thursday evening last, Mr. John
Cox, of this borough in his 50th year.

246. Dec 25 1827 (Tuesday) Died in this borough on Saturday last,
Mr. Peter Dinkle, in his 86th year.

247. Jan 1 1828 (Tuesday)
Married on Thursday last by R. Hamersly, Esq., Mr. John Grove to
  Miss Jane Bell, dau. of Mr. Ebenezer Bell, both of Warrington
  township, York Co.
- On Tuesday last by Rev. Reily, Mr. George P. Nevins to Miss
  Charlotte Hiss both of this town.
Died on Wednesday last in her 42nd year, Mrs. -- Kluge, consort of
  Rev. J. P. Kluge, Pastor of the Congregation of the United Brethren,
  in this borough.

248. Jan 8 1828 (Tuesday)
Married on Tuesday last by Rev. Reily, Dr. Abraham Bitner, of
  Washington, Lancaster Co., to Miss Helene Burkholthouse of Windsor
  township, York Co.
- On Thursday evening last by Rev. Kreber, Mr. Samuel Strayer to
  Miss Catharine Hanis, all of Dover township, York Co.
Died in this borough on Sunday evening last, Mrs. Ann Upp, consort of
  Mr. Jacob Upp, Jr. in her 24th year.

249. Jan 22 1828 (Tuesday) Died on Saturday evening the 19th
inst., William Nes, Esq., in his 68th year, past Treasurer of York Co.
and a member of the House of Representatives of the General
Assembly, also a successful merchant.

250. Jan 29 1828 (Tuesday)

Married on Thursday the 24th inst. by Rev. Reily, Mr. John Jacob Mayer to Miss Magdalene Kern, dau. of Mr. Frederick Kern.

- On the 25th by the same, Mr. Samuel Spangler to Miss Mary Wehlhaf.

- On the 27th by the same, Mr. George Cross to Miss Sarah Cumfort.

- On the 31st ult. in New Haven, (Conn.) Mr. Williams, aged 97, to Miss Polly Caudle, aged 14, both of Green River Hollow.

Died on Friday the 10th inst. in Hopewell township in his 78th year, Andrew Duncan, Esq., a church Elder and Magistrate of the commonwealth for almost 40 years.

- In this borough on Friday last, Mr. George Ilgenfritz, in his 37th year.

- On Saturday last, Mrs. Gertrude Moore, wife of Mr. Peter E. Moore of this borough in her 70th year.

251. Feb 5 1828 (Tuesday)

Died in this borough on Sunday last, Miss Elizabeth Lichty.

- On the same day, Margaret Koth, infant dau. of Mr. Richard Koth of this borough.

- At Lancaster on Wednesday last in her 22nd year, Miss Sarah Christiana Myer, dau. of Mr. John Myers formerly of this place.

252. Feb 12 1828 (Tuesday)

Married on the 7th inst by Rev. Hemphill, Mr. George Conn to Miss Catharine Angus, both of Margaretta Furnace, Windsor township.

Died on Saturday last in West Manchester township, Mrs. Barbara Baymiller, wife of Mr. George Baymiller in her 27th year.

253. Feb 19 1828 (Tuesday)

Died in this borough on Saturday last, Mr. Henry Phleeger.

- On the same day in his 18th year, Mr. Daniel Eurich.

254. Mar 4 1828 (Tuesday)

Married on Thursday last by Rev. Reily, Mr. Henry Feltenberger to Miss Anna Dugan.

- On the same day by the same, Mr. John Gates to Miss Elizabeth Feltenberger.

- On the same day by the same, Mr. Benjamin Myers of this borough to Miss Louisa Smyser, dau. of Mr. Jacob Smyser.

- On Sunday evening last by Rev. Kluge, Mr. Jacob Andrews to Miss Louisa Ruff, both of this borough.

255. Mar 11 1828 (Tuesday)
Married on Thursday last by Rev. Reily, Mr. George Solomon to Miss Elizabeth Eichholtz, both of Manchester township.
Died this morning in Marietta, Lancaster Co., Mr. William C. Carter, late a resident of this town.

256. Mar 18 1828 (Tuesday)
Married on Thursday last by Rev. Cathcart, Mr. John Manifold to Miss Miranda Meads, dau. of Benedict Meads, both of Hopewell township.
- On Thursday last by Rev. Reily, Mr. Robert Flint to Miss Sarah Bauer.
- In Columbia on Wednesday the 27th ult. by Rev. Boyer, Mr. John L. Wright to Miss Ann Evans, all of that place.
Died at Wrightsville, Pa., on the 25th ult., Mary Speer, dau. of Dr. Alexander Speer, in her 4th month.
- At New Holland on Tuesday last, Samuel Hough, son of Mr. Jonathan Hough in his 16th year.

257. Mar 25 1828 (Tuesday)
Married on Thursday last by Rev. Reily, Mr. George Byerts to Miss Maria Klatfelter.
Died in Lewistown, Pa., on Thursday the 13th inst., Ferdinand A. Melsheimer, formerly of this place.

258. Apr 1 1828 (Tuesday)
Died in this borough on Tuesday morning last, Mr. Daniel Fahs.
- On Friday morning last, Miss Matilda Minnich, dau. of the late Simon Minnich in her 15th year.

259. Apr 8 1828 (Tuesday) Died in this borough on Saturday last, Mr. David S. Cassat, eldest son of the late David Cassat, Esq., in his 30th year.

260. Apr 15 1828 (Tuesday) Married at Washington on the 9th inst by Rev. Johns, Thomas Jefferson Smith, Esq., Attorney at Law of New York, to Miss Louisa W. Myer, dau. of the late Major Solomon Myer, formerly of this borough.

261. Apr 22 1828 (Tuesday)
Married on Thursday the 18th last by Rev. Boyer, Mr. Thomas Hutton
to Miss Mary Stewart, both of Chanceford township.
- On Thursday the 17th by the same, Mr. James Adams to Miss Mary
Reese, both of this borough.
Died in this borough on Saturday evening last, Miss Harriett James,
youngest dau. of Mr. Nicholas James.
- In this borough on Friday last, Henry August Boyer, youngest son of
Rev. Stephen Boyer, in his 4th year.

262. Apr 29 1828 (Tuesday)
Married on Thursday last by Rev. Reily, Mr. George Frey to Miss
Rebecca Will.
- On the same day by the same, Mr. Peter Shultz to Miss Louisa
Spangler, dau. of Mr. Jesse Spangler.

263. May 6 1828 (Tuesday) Married on Thursday evening the 24th
ult. by Rev. Hall, Mr. George Jacobs to Miss Mary Gipe, all of this
borough.

264. May 13 1828 (Tuesday)
Married on Sunday evening last by Rev. Stephen Boyer, Mr. George
Lloyd to Mrs. Elizabeth Lutman, both of this borough.
- On Thursday last by Rev. J. R. Reily, Mr. George Liebenstein to Miss
Elizabeth Roemer.
Died on Saturday in Spring Garden township, Mrs. -- Miller, wife of
Mr. Christian Miller.

265. May 27 1828 (Tuesday) Married on Thursday last by Rev. J. R.
Reily, Mr. George Baer to Miss Sarah Smyser, dau. of Mr. Peter
Smyser.

266. Jun 3 1828 (Tuesday)
Married in this borough on Saturday the 24th ult. by Rev. J. P. Kluge,
Mr. John Markey, age 75, to Miss Rosina Bleymier, age 30, both of
York Co.
- On Wednesday last by Rev. Stephen Boyer, Mr. William D. Ramsay,
Esq., to Miss Charlotte Arnold, both of Adams Co.

267. Jun 26 1828 (Tuesday)
Married on Sunday evening last by Rev. Schmucker, Mr. Jeremiah
Trexler to Miss Charlotte Wearley, both of this borough.
- At Lancaster on Tuesday last by Rev. Joseph Clarkson, Dr. Jacob
Glatz, of Marietta, Lancaster Co., to Miss Susan Hiestand, dau. of
Abraham Hiestand of this county.
Died in this borough on Wednesday last, Mrs. Sarah Ilgenfritz, relict of
Mr. George Ilgenfritz dec'd. in her 33rd year.
- Yesterday Mr. Henry Weiser in his 50th year.

268. Jul 1 1828 (Tuesday)
Married in this borough on Tuesday last by Rev. Boyer, Mr. George
Caracher to Miss Mary Saylor, both of Marietta.
- At Lancaster on Wednesday last, Mr. John Crout of Lancaster, to
Miss Susan Landis, of this borough.
Died on Thursday last in this borough in his 81st year, Thomas
Randolph, better known as "Old Tommy Randals", a soldier of the
Revolution.

269. Jul 15 1828 (Tuesday)
Married on Thursday evening last by Rev. Kluge, Mr. Jacob Spangler
to Miss Ann Zorger, both of this borough.
Died on Wednesday morning last in his 41st year, Mr. Daniel Billmyer,
for many years editor of "Wahre Republikaner."

270. Jul 22 1828 (Tuesday)
Married on Thursday evening last by Rev. J. R. Reily, Mr. Martin
Austin to Miss Mary Cramer, dau. of Mr. Jacob Cramer, both of this
borough.
Died on Thursday the 17th inst. Mr. John Mann of Hellam township in
his 98th year.

271. Jul 29 1828 (Tuesday)
Married on Thursday last by Rev. J. R. Riley, Mr. George Menges to
Miss Margaret Emig.
- On the same day by the same, Mr. William Krouse to Miss Eliza
Musselman.

272. Aug 5 1828 (Tuesday)   Died on Wednesday morning last in York
township, Miss Ruth Tipton in her 24th year.

273. Aug 12 1828 (Tuesday)
Married on Thursday last by Rev. J. R. Reily, Mr. John Bear to Miss
    Mary Hershy.
- At Philadelphia on Thursday last, Mr. George Hoke, of West
    Manchester, to Miss Kendricks, of the former place.

274. Aug 19 1828 (Tuesday)
Died on Sunday night, Ignatius Leitner, Esq., at an advanced age of
    this borough.
- On the same day at an advanced age, Mr. Frederick Hibner, a soldier
    of the Revolution and a native of Germany.

275. Sep 9 1828 (Tuesday)   Died a few days since at Pittsburg, Pa.,
Mr. James Scanlan, formerly of this place.

276. Sep 16 1828 (Tuesday)   Died on Saturday the 13th inst. Jacob
Heckart, Esq., in his 70th year in this borough, former Justice of the
Peace, Commissioner of York Co. and member of Penn. Legislature.

277. Sep 23 1828 (Tuesday)
Married on Sunday last by Rev. J. R. Reily, Mr. Christian Roth to Miss
    Juliana Fritz, both of Spring garden.
Died on the 12th inst. in this county, Samuel Jordan, Esq., formerly a
    member of Pennsylvania Legislature.

278. Oct 7 1828 (Tuesday)   Died in this borough on Tuesday last,
Mrs. Catharine Kraber, wife of Rev. Kraber.

279. Oct 21 1828 (Tuesday)   Died near this borough on Sunday night
last, Mr. William Johnson, a member of the Washington Artillerists, in
his 23rd year.

280. Oct 28 1828 (Tuesday)
Died on Friday morning last, Mr. William Heckman, a native of
    Germany, for many years a resident of this borough in his 48th year.
- At New Orleans on the 12th of Aug last, Mr. Alexander Cahoon,
    formerly of this place in his 26th year.
- Yesterday in this borough, Mr. George Leitner.
Married on Thursday last by Rev. J. R. Reily, Mr. Daniel Bair to Miss
    Susanna Hershy, both of Codorus township.

281. Nov 4 1828 (Tuesday)
Married on Thursday evening last by Rev. J. R. Reily, Mr. Henry
  Reisinger to Miss Catharine Good, both of this borough.
Died in this borough on Thursday evening last, Mrs. Sarah Truett, wife
  of Mr. John Truett in her 21st year.
- On Saturday last in this borough, Catharine Klinefelter, dau. of Mr.
  Adam Klinefelter.

282. Nov 11 1828 (Tuesday)   Died on the 13th ult. in Mont Alto
Furnace in this county, Mrs. Mary Stoops, at the advanced age of 117
years.

283. Nov 18 1828 (Tuesday)
Died on Saturday last in Springgarden township, Mrs. Ferree, wife of
  Mr. Andrew Ferree in her 65th year.
- In Buttstown on Saturday last, Mrs. Bupp, wife of Mr. Jacob Bupp.

284. Nov 25 1828 (Tuesday)
Married on Thursday evening last by Rev. Schmucker, Mr. John
  Roffinsberger of Paradise, to Miss Catharine Lochner, of this
  borough.
- On the same day by Rev. J. R. Reily, Mr. Jacob Emig to Mrs.
  Catharine Ferree, dau. of Jacob Lauks.
- On Sunday the 23rd inst. by the same, Mr. Jacob Lauks, Sr. to Miss
  Elizabeth Peter.
Died in Lancaster on Sunday evening the 16th inst., Mr. Philip Myer,
  formerly of this borough in his 80th year.
- In Wrightsville on Tuesday last, Mr. Philip Duffield in his 39th year.
- In Springgarden township on Thursday last, Mr. Isaac Grove in his
  60th year.
- Yesterday morning in this borough, Mr. Charles Kurtz, merchant, in
  his 38th year.

285. Dec 9 1828 (Tuesday)
Married on the 4th inst by Rev. J. G. Kraber, Mr. Samuel Ryde to Miss
  Lydia Friess, both of this county.
- On Thursday last by Rev. J. R. Reily, Mr. Henry Raymer to Miss
  Margaret Smith, of this borough.
- On Sunday last by the same, Mr. Henry Brigle to Miss Catharine
  Reynolds, both of this borough.

Died on Wednesday last in this borough, Mr. Samuel Schultz, in his
24th year.
- On the 20th ult. in Windsor township, Anthony Hines, Esq., in his
87th year.
- On Thursday the 4th inst. at Mechanicsburg, Cumberland Co., Mr.
Samuel Jackson, formerly a resident of this borough.

286. Dec 23 1828 (Tuesday)
Died in this borough on Sunday morning last, Mr. Andrew Neuman in
his 60th year.
- On Friday the 12th inst. in Freystown, Mr. John Lehr in his 50th
year.

287. Jan 6 1829 (Tuesday)
Married on Wednesday last by Rev. J. R. Reily, Mr. John Schroll to
Miss Judith Bear, all of this county.
- On Thursday by the same, Mr. Daniel Reinoll to Miss Martha Hutton,
of Warrington township.
- At Marietta on Monday the 29th ult. by Rev. Douglass, Mr. Peter E.
Moore, Jr. to Miss Henrietta Kluge, dau. of Rev. J. P. Kluge, of this
borough.
Died on Wednesday last in this borough, Mr. Jacob Stuck in his 76th
year.

288. Jan 13 1829 (Tuesday)
Married on the 4th inst. by Rev. Schmucker, Mr. George Fisher to
Miss Catharine Yesslen.
- On Thursday last by Rev. J. R. Reily, Mr. Peter Zacharias, of
Washington Co., Md., to Miss Barbara King, youngest dau. of Philip
J. King, Esq., of Springgarden township, York Co.
- On the 1st inst. at Lancaster by Rev. Becker, Dr. Elisha Hallowell, of
Windsor township York Co., to Miss Elizabeth Brabson of Columbia.
Died at Baltimore on the 1st inst. Dr. Charles Julian Joseph Pochon, a
native of Arras, France, and for some year a practicing physician in
this borough.

289. Jan 20 1829 (Tuesday)   Died in this borough on Tuesday last,
Mr. Joseph W. Webb in his 23rd year.

290. Feb 3 1829 (Tuesday)
Married on Tuesday last by Rev. Zacharias, Mr. Jacob Schafer to Miss
Harriet Wineholdt, both of York township.
- On Thursday by the same, Mr. John Hake, of Manchester, to Miss
Maria Patton, of Dover.
- On the 20th ult. by James Johnston, Esq., Mr. John Cunningham to
Miss Margaret Grimes, both of Lower Chanceford.
Died at Milton, Pa., on the 26th ult. Daniel Scudder, Esq., former
member of Pennsylvania Legislature.

291. Feb 10 1829 (Tuesday)
Married on Tuesday the 27th ult. by Rev. F. W. Vondersloodt, Mr.John
Williams to Miss Rebecca Rensel.
- On Thursday the 29th ult. by the same, Mr. John Rensel to Miss
Rebecca Baker.
- On the same day by the same, Mr. Jacob Jacobs to Miss Sarah
Altland.
- On the same day by the same, Mr. David Schwartz to Miss Lydia
Spangler.
- On the same day by the same, Mr. Daniel Baab to Miss Lydia Clark.
- On the same day by the same, Mr. Jesse Spangler to Miss ---
Eichelberger.
- On the same day, at Bethlehem, by Rev. Bishop Anders, the Rev. J.
P. Kluge of this borough to Miss Mary Eliza Albright, dau. of Mr.
Henry Albright, of Nazareth.
Died on Wednesday morning last, in Chanceford township, York Co.
Mr. James Adams in his 63rd year.

292. Feb 24 1829 (Tuesday)
Married at Columbia on 22nd inst. by Rev. Stephen Boyer, Mr. David
Hyde to Miss Barbara Shonk, both of Lancaster Co.
Died on Sunday the 15th inst near Oxford, Adams Co., Rev. John F.
Melsheimer, for Pastor of Lutheran Congregation at Hanover in his
46th year.
- On Thursday morning in this borough, Mr. Spangler Koons, in his
28th year.
- On Saturday night in West Manchester township, Mr. Matthias
Smyser, Sr. in his 84th year.
- In Dillsburg, York Co., on Thursday last, Mr. William Chambers.

293. Mar 3 1829 (Tuesday)   Died yesterday in Springgarden township, Mr. Philip J. King in his 65th year.

294. Mar 17 1829 (Tuesday)
Married on Sunday evening last by Rev. Richard D. Hall, Mr. William Griffith to Miss Sarah Gotwalt, both of this borough.
Died on Saturday evening, Mr. Henry Snyder, formerly of Philadelphia, but for several years a resident of this borough in his 43rd year.
- At Harrisburg on Monday the 9th inst., John De'Pui, Esq., Clerk of Senate of Pa.

295. Mar 24 1829 (Tuesday)
Died on Thursday evening at Gettysburg the 12th inst., Dr. Thomas B. Cobean in his 32nd year.
- At Hanover on Wednesday evening last, Mr. Joseph Schmuck, former publisher of the Hanover Guardian.
- At Harrisburg on the 17th inst., Samuel Mifflin, Esq., President of the Union Canal Company.
- On Sunday last in Hellam township, York Co., Mr. Conrad Dietz in his 60th year.

296. Mar 31 1829 (Tuesday)
Married on Sunday evening last by Rev. Schmucker, Mr. James Littel to Miss Elizabeth Smith, both of this borough.
Died on Thursday last in West Manchester township, Mr. Elias Eyster in his 98th year.
- On the same day in Baltimore, Md., Mr. Martin Kraber in his 72nd year, formerly a resident of this place.
- On Saturday in this borough Mrs. Hays at an advanced age.
- On the same day at Harrisburg, Eben S. Kelly, Esq., member of the Pennsylvania Senate from Indiana Co.
- On the same day at the same place, Dr. William Lehman, a distinguished member of the House of Representatives from Philadelphia.
- On Sunday morning in his 75th year, Mr. Christian Hildebrand, Sr. of this borough.

297. Apr 7 1829 (Tuesday)
Married on Thursday evening last by Rev. Schmucker, Mr. Alexander Reisinger, of Buttstown, to Miss Margaret Schriver of this borough.

- On Sunday evening last by Rev. Smith, Mr. Martin Basehore to Miss
Susanna Pierce, both of this borough.

Died at Columbus on Saturday morning last, Mr. John Wolff, formerly
of this place.

- In this borough yesterday morning, Mrs. Mary Baymiller at an
advanced age.

298. Apr 14 1829 (Tuesday)
Married on Tuesday last by Rev. Schmucker, Mr. Abraham
Baumgardner of this borough to Miss Sarah Eichelberger, dau. of Mr.
Barnet Eichelberger dec'd. of West Manchester township.

Died on Wednesday last in West Manchester township in her 24th
year, Mrs. Elizabeth Loucks, dau. of Mr. Matthias Smyser.

299. Apr 21 1829 (Tuesday)
Married at Lancaster on Thursday last by Rev. Baker, Mr. George
Bahm to Miss Lydia Kauffman, both of this county.

Died at Lancaster on Tuesday morning last, Ebenezer Wright, Esq.,
Counsellor at Law in his 50th year.

- In this borough on Thursday evening last, Mr. Jacob Shultz in his
33rd year.

300. Apr 28 1829 (Tuesday)
Married on Thursday evening last by Rev. Kluge, Mr. Daniel Cremer,
of this borough, to Miss Mary Reisinger, of Buttstown.

- On Sunday last by Rev. Stecker, Mr. Jacob Cremer, Jr. to Miss
Catharine Weaver, dau. of Mr. Daniel Weaver, all of this borough.

301. May 5 1829 (Tuesday)
Died on Tuesday last in West Manchester township, Mr. Cornelius
Garretson in his 73rd year.

- On Sunday morning last in this borough, Mrs. Lydia Wolff in her 39th
year.

- In Monaghan township on the 23rd ult., Mr. John Cavenaugh, in his
80th year, an officer of the Revolutionary army serving from the
beginning of the war to its close.

- On Monday of last week near Havre de Grace, Md., in his 59th year,
Mr. Peter Hoke, of Buttstown.

302. May 19 1829 (Tuesday)

Married on Tuesday last by Rev. J. R. Reily, Mr. Jacob Strickler to Miss Rebecca Smith, both of West Manchester township.

- On Sunday last by the same, Mr. Samuel Spangler to Miss Elizabeth Frank, both of this borough.
- On the 12th inst. near Mercersburg by Rev. Elliot, Francis Wyeth, Esq., Editor of the Harrisburg Argus to Miss Susan B. Maxwell, dau. of Mr. William Maxwell of Franklin Co.

Died on Saturday last in Manchester township in her 50th year, Mrs. Anna Maria Emig, wife of John Emig (of Valentine.)

-Yesterday morning in this borough, Mrs. Leah Schroeder, wife of Mr. Emanuel H. Schroeder.

303. May 26 1829 (Tuesday)

Married on Sunday the 17th inst at New Cumberland by Rev. Sprigg, Mr. Abraham Ilgenfritz to Miss Catharine Tyler, both of this borough.

- On Thursday last at Lancaster, Mr. Jonas Hamme, of Dover township, to Miss Catharine Eisenhart, dau. of Mr. George Eisenhart of West Manchester.

Died on Wednesday in this borough in his 37th year, Mr. George W. Spangler.

304. Jun 2 1829 (Tuesday)

Married on Tuesday the 26th inst. Mr. James M. Griggs, of Baltimore, to Miss Abegail Potts of Newberry township, York Co.

- On Thursday last by Rev. Zacharias, Mr. John Kinder to Miss Lydia Miller, both of this county.

Died in this borough on Saturday evening last, Mr. Francis Campbell, a native of Ireland.

- Recently at Rochester, N.Y., Mr. Samuel Bahn of Hellam township in this county.

305. Jun 9 1829 (Tuesday)

Married on Thursday last by Rev. Zacharias, Mr. William Krepper to Miss Julian Ruby.

Died on Thursday last in Hellam township, Mr. Joseph Bahn in his 34th year.

306. Jun 16 1829 (Tuesday)
Married on Sunday evening last by Rev. J. P. Kluge, Mr. Henry
Armprister to Miss Anna Mary Beck, dau. of Mr. Jacob Beck, all of
this borough.
- On the 7th inst. by Rev. J. R. Reily, Mr. Frederick Shafer to Miss
Mary Bitner, both of this county.
- On Wednesday last by Rev. D. Zacharias, Mr. Edward Carven to Miss
Mary Scheckles.
- On Thursday by the same, Mr. Daniel Tyson to Miss Elizabeth
Hammer, all of this county.
Died on Thursday last in Springgarden township, Mr. John Meyer in
his 67th year.

307. Jun 23 1829 (Tuesday) Died yesterday in this borough, Mrs.
Sarah Christine, wife of Mr. Jacob Christine.

308. Jun 30 1829 (Tuesday) Married on Thursday morning last by
Rev. Geo. Duffield, the Rev. Daniel Zacharias, of this place, to Miss
Jane Hays, dau. of Joseph Hays, Esq., of Carlisle.

309. Jul 14 1829 (Tuesday)
Married on Thursday the 2nd inst. by Rev. Goforth, the Rev. John
Lenhart, of Dauphin, to Mrs. Ann Poor, of York Haven.
- On the 25th ult. by Mr. Morrisson, Col. Hugh Ross, of Lower
Chanceford, York Co., to Miss Rebecca Glenn, dau. of Mr. William
Glenn, of Harford Co., Md.
Died on the 24th ult. at Canton, Ohio, Mr. Abner Davis, late of York,
in his 24th year.
- On Sunday in this borough, Mr. John Keefer, Sr.

310. Jul 21 1829 (Tuesday)
Married on Sunday last by Rev. Stephen Boyer, Mr. Jacob Naggle to
Miss Ann Runk, both of Mountjoy township, Lancaster Co.
Died on the 10th inst. in Hopewell township at an advanced age, Mr.
Abraham Miller.
- On Wednesday last in West Manchester township in her 19th year,
Miss Mary Smyser, dau. of Mr. Daniel Smyser.
- On Thursday last in this borough in her 74th year, Mrs. -- Shetter,
widow of Mr. Martin Shetter, dec'd. of Newbury township.

- On Saturday in Baltimore Co., Md., in her 33rd year, Mrs. Sarah Smyser, wife of Mr. Adam Smyser, innkeeper.
- On Saturday morning last in Springgarden township, Mrs. Margaret Lehr, wife of Mr. John Lehr, dec'd.

311. Jul 28 1829 (Tuesday) Married on Thursday last by Rev. D. Zacharias, Mr. Jacob Hinckley, of Wrightsville, to Miss Leah Krohn, of Hellam township.

312. Aug 4 1829 (Tuesday)
Married on Tuesday the 21st ult. by Isaac Kirk, Esq., Mr. James Nichols, merchant, to Miss Mary Ann Blymoyer, all of Lewisberry.
Died on Thursday last in this borough, Mr. Jacob Pflieger in his 73rd year.
- On Tuesday in Buttstown, Mr. William Slagle, formerly of Gettysburg, in his 21st year.

313. Aug 11 1829 (Tuesday)
Married on Tuesday last by Rev. D. Zacharias, Mr. Peter Dohm to Miss Elizabeth Schmeltzer, both of Windsor township.
- On Thursday last by the same, Mr. George Matthias to Miss Catharine May, both of Conewago township.
- On the same day by the same, Mr. Isaac Baumgartner to Miss Joanna Pentz, both of this place.

314. Aug 18 1829 (Tuesday)
Married at Baltimore on Thursday the 6th inst. by Rev. Joseph Fry, Mr. Samuel Thompson, of this county, to Miss Sarah Ann Coady, formerly of York, Pa.
Died on Thursday last in this borough in his 78th year, Mr. Philip Waltemeyer.
- On Tuesday the 4th inst. near Harrisburg, Jacob Bomberger in his 85th year.

315. Aug 25 1829 (Tuesday)
Married on Wednesday the 12th inst. by Rev. D. Zacharias, Mr. Francis Sims to Miss Sarah Turk, both of this county.
- On Tuesday morning last by Rev. Boyer, Mr. George Webb of Baltimore, to Miss Margaret L. Willis, of this borough.

316. Sep 1 1829 (Tuesday)
Married on Thursday the 19th ult. by Rev. J. Oswald, Mr. Peter
Westheffer to Miss Ann Maria Stair, both of this county.
Died on Sunday evening last at an advanced age, Mr. John Beaty, a
soldier of the revolution.

317. Sep 8 1829 (Tuesday) Married at Lancaster on Thursday
evening last by Rev. Bowman, Mr. Ferdinand L. Spangler of this place,
to Miss Delia Amanda Wright, eldest dau. of late Ebenezer Wright,
Esq., of Lancaster.

318. Sep 15 1829 (Tuesday)
Married on Thursday last by Rev. J. R. Reily, Mr. Abraham Hiestand,
Jr. to Miss Leah Longenecker, both of Springgarden.
- On Tuesday last in Hopewell township by John Smith, Esq., Mr.
Jacob Dailey to Miss Rosanna Zellars, both of said township.
Died on Saturday the 5th inst in her 19th year, Miss Martha Porter,
only dau. of Mr. James Porter of Monaghan township, York Co.

319. Sep 22 1829 (Tuesday)
Married on the 8th inst. by Rev. Schmucker, Mr. Abraham Hess to
Miss Maria Sandoe, both of Lancaster Co.
- On the 17th inst. by the same, Mr. Peter Dessenberg to Miss Anna
Maria Welty, both of Manchester township.
Died in Dover township on the 16th inst. in his 85th year, Mr. William
Teklodt, formerly of this borough.

320. Sep 29 1829 (Tuesday)
Married on the 27th inst. by Rev. D. Zacharias, Mr. George Heindel to
Miss Leah Wineholdt, both of this county.
- On the 7th inst. by the same, Mr. Peter Ruby to Miss Clementine
Green, both of Washington, Lancaster Co.
- On Tuesday the 22nd inst. by Rev. S. Boyer, Mr. L. Anderson to Miss
Rebecca Morthland.
- On Sunday evening last by Rev. Schmucker, Mr. Henry Ginter to
Miss Maria Smith, dau. of Mr. Robert Smith, all of this borough.

321. Oct 6 1829 (Tuesday)
Married at Gettysburg on Thursday last, Mr. Thomas B. Schall to Miss
Eliza Spangler, both of this borough.

- In Codorus township by Rev. Andrew Miller, Mr. David Miller, of Manheim, to Miss Elizabeth Petry, of Codorus.
Died in this borough on Thursday last, Mr. Daniel Cookes, in his 17th year.
- On Friday last in this borough, Mr. Jacob Keefer in his 22nd year.
- In Manchester township on Friday last, Mrs. Landis, wife of Mr. Daniel Landis.

322. Oct 13 1829 (Tuesday)
Married on Tuesday last by Rev. Reily, Mr. Henry Miller to Miss Margaret Weigel, both of Dover township.
- On the same day by Rev. Jacob Shepherd, Mr. Thomas Henderson of Harford Co., Md., to Miss Jane Lutes of York Co.
- On Sunday evening last by Rev. J. P. Kluge, Mr. Jacob Christine to Mrs. Margaret Harman, both of this place.
- At Baltimore on the 5th inst by Rev. Henshaw, Mr. Samuel Hopkins, merchant of Baltimore, to Miss Elizabeth Kelley, eldest dau. of late James Kelley, Esq., of this borough.
Died on Wednesday evening last in Pottstown in his 62nd year, Mr. Martin Eichelberger.
- On Monday evening in this borough, Mr. John Horn, in his 83rd year, a solider of the Revolution.

323. Oct 20 1829 (Tuesday)
Married on Thursday evening last by Rev. Smith, Mr. John Covode, of Westmoreland Co., Pa., to Miss Sarah Hay, dau. of Col. George Hay of this borough.
- At Lewisberry on Sunday evening the 11th inst. by Isaac Kirk, Esq., Mr. John H. Kaufman of Fairview township to Miss Phebe Griffith of Lewisberry.

324. Oct 27 1829 (Tuesday)
Married on Tuesday last by Rev. J. R. Reily, Mr. George Graver to Miss Rebecca Filby, both of this borough.
- On Sunday last by Rev. J. Reily, Samuel Johnston, Esq., of Springgarden to Miss Mary Smyser, dau. of Mr. Michael Smyser, of West Manchester.
- On the 18th inst. at Marietta, Mr. David Wilson, of Shrewsbury township, to Miss Eliza Glenn, of Marietta.

- On Thursday evening last by Rev. J. P. Kluge, Mr. Jacob Bopp, to Mrs. Mary Cremer both of Bottstown.
- At York Haven on Thursday the 22nd inst. by Rev. Cathcart, Dr. J. G. Shoch, formerly of Harrisburg, to Miss Ann Maria Jacobs, dau. of late Capt. Wilson Jacobs, of Baltimore.

Died in this borough on Thursday evening last, Mr. Martin J. Weiser in his 41st year.
- In this borough on Friday evening last, Mr. John Nicholas in his 22nd year.

325. Nov 10 1829 (Tuesday)
Married on the 27th ult. by Rev. Smith, Joseph Morris, Esq., to Mrs. Mary Nailor, both of this borough.
- On the 8th inst. by Rev. J. R. Reily, Mr. Henry Mayer to Miss Barbara Hershy, both of this county.

Died on Friday morning last in this borough in his 47th year, Daniel Heckert, Esq.

326. Nov 17 1829 (Tuesday)
Married at Dillsburg on the 4th Nov by Rev. Keplar, Mr. William Marks to Miss Mary Burns, eldest dau. of Mr. Francis Burns.
- On Tuesday last by Rev. Deininger, Mr. Wm. Smyser to Miss Catharine Petsel, youngest dau. of Mr. Abraham Petsel of Dillsburgh.
- On Thursday last at Mechanicsburg, Cumberland Co. by Rev. Williamson, Mr. James G. Frazer, merchant, to Miss Sarah M'Guire, youngest dau. of late Peter M'Guire, both of Dillsburg.
- On Thursday evening last by Rev. J. R. Reily, Mr. George Winebrenner, of Hanover, to Mrs. Mary Danner, of this borough.

327. Nov 24 1829 (Tuesday)
Married on Tuesday evening last by Rev. Cathcart, Rev. Alexander McCahon of Chambersburg to Miss Sarah Ann Boyer, eldest dau. of Rev. Stephen Boyer of this borough.
- On Tuesday the 17th inst. by Rev. J. R. Kesher, Mr. John Mann, Jr. to Miss Elizabeth Blessing, dau. of Mr. Philip Blessing, all of Hellam township.
- On the 8th inst. by Rev. D. Zacharias, Mr. George Albright to Miss Rebecca Summers, both of this borough.
- At Morristown, N. J. on the 11th inst. by Rev. A. Barnes, the Rev. Daniel Young, Assistant Professor in the Theological Seminary at this

place, to Mrs. Sarah Ann Pearson, dau. of Mr. L. Moore, merchant of
the former place.
- On the 22nd inst. by Rev. D. Schmucker, Mr. Jacob Liebenstein to
Miss Ann Maria Fissel, both of this county.
- On the 18th inst. by the same, Mr. Isaac Bowman to Miss Mary Baer,
both of Lancaster Co.
Died in Philadelphia on 28th Sept in her 99th year, Mrs. Jane
M'Calmond, for many years a resident of York, Pa.

328. Dec 1 1829 (Tuesday)
Married on Thursday evening last by Rev. Cathcart, David Lamott,
Esq., to Miss Eliza Williams, dau. of Mr. John F. Williams, all of this
borough.
- On the same evening by Rev. Smith, Mr. William Coulter to Miss
Rebecca Welsh, dau. of Mr. John Welsh, butcher of this borough.
- On the same evening by the same, Mr. Joseph McPherson to Mrs.
Rachael Hunter, both of this borough.
- On the 28th inst. by Rev. Schmucker, Mr. John Jacob Keller to Miss
Christiana R. Bodenhoefer, both of this borough.
- On the 29th inst. by the same, Mr. Josiah Tracey to Miss Ann
Furrell, both of Hellam township.
- On Wednesday evening the 10th inst. in Adams Co. by Rev. D.
M'Conaughy, Col. James L. Neely, of Tyrone township, to Miss Sarah
Y. Cassat; and on the same evening by the same, Mr. John Neely, of
Tyrone township, to Miss Hannah F. Cassat, both dau. of Jacob
Cassat, Esq. of Straban township.
Died on Wednesday morning last in his 30th year, John Bowie, Esq.,
Attorney at Law, son of late Ralph Bowie, Esq., formerly a lawyer of
this place.
- On Thursday evening last in this borough in her 52nd year, Mrs.
Elizabeth Platts, wife of Mr. Thomas Platts of this borough.
- At Philadelphia on Thursday last in his 71st year, the Hon. Bushrod
Washington, Judge of the Supreme Court of the United States.

329. Dec 8 1829 (Tuesday)
Died at Dillsburg, York Co. on the 25th Nov, Mr. Samuel M'Ilhenny,
son of James M'Ilhenny, Sr. of Mountjoy township in his 35th year.
- On the 28th ult. in her 60th year near Philadelphia, Mrs. Anne
Washington, relict of the Hon. Bushrod Washington, dec'd.

- At Philadelphia, on Wednesday last in his 32nd year, the Rev. William Ashmead, late pastor of Presbyterian Congregation in Lancaster.

330. Dec 15 1829 (Tuesday) Died at York Haven on Saturday the 5th inst. Mr. John Poor in his 78th year.

331. Dec 29 1829 (Tuesday)
Married on Thursday evening last by Rev. Schmucker, Mr. Samuel Ilgenfritz, Jr. to Miss Eliza Weiser, dau. of Mr. Samuel Weiser, all of this borough.
- On the same evening by the same, Mr. Lewis Smith to Miss Louisa She(?), both of this borough.

332. Jan 5 1830 (Tuesday)
Married on Friday morning last by Rev. Mayer, Mr. Strapp, of Carlisle, to Miss Catharine Swartzbach of this borough.
- At Lewisberry on Thursday the 31st ult. by Isaac Kirk, Esq., Mr. Daniel Kauffman to Miss Eliza Wilson, both of Lewisberry.

333. Feb 2 1830 (Tuesday)
Married on Thursday evening last by Rev. J. Oswald, Dr. Thomas Stevens of Berlin, Adams Co., to Mrs. Helenah Doudel, dau. of Mr. John Demuth of this borough.
- On Thursday evening the 21st ult. by Rev. Boyer, Mr. Samuel Zink to Miss Mary Spencer both of Lancaster Co.
Died at Williamsport, Pa., on the 20th ult. in his 74th year, Mr. Abraham Graffius, formerly of this place.

334. Feb 9 1830 (Tuesday)
Married on Tuesday the 26th ult. at Shepherdstown, Va., by Rev. Mathews, Mr. Thornton C. Dunham to Miss Louisa Worley, dau. of Mr. Joseph Worley, formerly of this place.
Died on Wednesday the 27th ult. in Shrewsbury township, Mr. Lawrence Kleinfelter in his 93rd year.

335. Feb. 16 1830 (Tuesday) Married on Thursday evening last by Rev. Reily, Mr. Joseph Ruby to Miss Sarah Barnhart, all of this place.

336. Feb 23 1830 (Tuesday) Died in this borough on Sunday morning last, Mr. John Myers.

337. Mar 2 1830 (Tuesday)
Married on Thursday last by Rev. Stephen Boyer, Mr. Robert
Fullerton, Jr. to Miss Mary Crone.
Died in this borough yesterday morning, Mr. Job Bacon in his 35th
year.

338. Mar 9 1830 (Tuesday) Died on Saturday morning, Frederick
Manning Wadsworth, Esq., Counsellor at Law, a native of Pittsfield,
Mass. aged between 35 and 40 years.

INDEX

-A-
ABEL, George, 8
 Miss, 8
ADAMS, James, 50, 55
AHL, Daniel, 9, 17, 38
 George Washington, 38
 Mrs., 9
ALBERT, Rev., 45
ALBRIGHT, George, 63
 Henry, 55
 Mary Eliza, 55
ALLBRIGHT, Henry, 8
ALLEN, Rev., 46
ALRICKS, James, 43
ANDERS, Rev. Bishop, 55
ANDERSON, James, 25
 L., 61
 Mary, 25
ANDREWS, Jacob, 49
ANGUS, Catharine, 48
ANTHONY, Joseph B., 7
ARMPRISTER, Henry, 59
ARMSTRONG, John, 44
 William, 36
ARNOLD, Charlotte, 50
 Maria, 37
ARTHUR, Elizabeth, 13
ASHMEAD, William, 65
ATLAND, Sarah, 55
AUGHINBAUGH, J., 30
 Levi, 30

AUGUSTINE,
 Catharine, 9
 Simon, 9
AUSTIN, Martin, 51
AXE, Adam, 41

-B-
BAAB, Daniel, 55
BACON, Job, 66
BAER, Gabriel, 28
 George, 50
 Mary, 64
BAHM, George, 57
BAHN, Jacob, 37
 Joseph, 58
 Samuel, 58
BAILETS, Elizabeth, 14
 William, 14
BAILOR, John, 41
BAIR, Daniel, 52
BAKER, Catharine, 6
 Rebecca, 55
 Rev., 57
BARLAND, Andrew, 36
BARNES, A., 63
BARNHART, Elizabeth, 14
 Sarah, 65
BARNISE, William, 8
BARNITZ, Catharine, 26
 Catherine, 30
 Daniel, 21
 George, 26, 39
 John, 30
 Samuel, 19
BARNUM, David S., 45
BARRETT, Eliza, 16

BARRY, Rev., 32, 34, 37, 41
BARTH, Peter D., 30
BASEHORE, Martin, 57
BAUER, Sarah, 49
BAUGHER, Frederick, 44
BAUMGARDNER
 Abraham, 57
 John, 5
 Mrs., 5
BAUMGARTNER,
 Isaac, 60
BAXTER, Jane, 40
BAYER, Rev., 37
BAYMILLER, Barbara, 48
 George, 48
 Mary, 57
BEAR, John, 52
 Judith, 54
BEARD, Emily, 4
 Michael, 4, 21
 William, 31
BEATTY, James, 32
BEATY, Agness, 22
 John, 61
 William, 22
BECK, Anna Mary, 59
 Jacob, 59
 John, 24, 26
BECKER, Jacob, 35
 Rev., 54
BEHA, Bernard, 41
BEITZEL, Louisa, 3
BEITZELL, Elizabeth, 39
BELL, Ebenezer, 47

Jane, 47
BENTZ, F., 12
Frederick, 12
George, 46
John, 46
Maria, 46
Peter, 17
BIDDLE, Valeria, 21
William M., 21
BIERMAN, Abraham, 4
Mary, 4
BILLET, Jacob, 8
BILLMEYER,
Elizabeth, 20
BILLMYER, Daniel, 51
BITNER, Adam, 12
Catharine, 12
Dr. Abraham, 47
Jacob, 10
Mary, 59
BLESSING, Elizabeth,
63
Philip, 63
BLEYMIER, Rosina, 50
BLYMOYER, Mary
Ann, 60
BODENHOEFER,
Christiana R., 64
BOFAENG, Catharine
B., 10
BOGGS, William, 18
BOMBERGER, Jacob,
60
BOPP, Jacob, 63
BOTT, Jacob, 16
BOWERS, Elizabeth, 11
Jacob, 11
BOWIE, Deborah M.,
18
John, 64

Ralph, 18, 64
BOWMAN, Benjamin,
26
Henry, 31
Isaac, 64
Rev., 61
BOYD, Stephen, 2
BOYER, Elizabeth, 38
Henry, 38
Henry August, 50
John, 28
Mrs., 31
Rev., 8, 18, 30, 40, 49,
50, 51, 60, 65
Rev. Mr., 2
S., 34, 61
Stephen, 31, 43, 50,
55, 59, 63, 66
Sarah Ann, 63
BRABSON, Elizabeth,
54
BRENISE, Elizabeth,
16
John, 40
BRETZ, Elizabeth, 26
BRICKLE, John, 42
BRIGLE, Henry, 53
BROOKS, Samuel, 9, 12
BROWN, John, 32
Sarah, 26
William, 16
BRUCKHART, Daniel,
27
Mary, 27
BRYSON, Rev., 13
BUATT, Joseph, 27
BUCHANAN, James, 3
BUCHER, Hon. Jacob,
46
BUCKIUS, John, 37

BUEHLER, Fanny, 34
BUEHYLER, Ann
Mary, 44
BUEL, Maria, 25
Sarah, 6
William, 6, 25
BUGLEY, Rachel, 33
BUPP, Catherine, 8
Jacob, 53
Mrs., 53
BURKHAUSER, Sarah,
34
BURKHOLTHOU SE,
Helene, 47
BURNS, Fancis, 63
Mary, 63
BUSER, Jacob, 40
Mary, 40
BUYER, Jacob, 9
BYERTS, George, 49

-C-
CABUTE, John, 34
CAHOON, Alexander,
52
CAMERON, John, 15
Robert, 4
CAMP, Rev., 6
CAMPBELL, Francis,
58
CARACHER, George,
51
CARR, William, 2
CARTER, B., 21
Julianna, 21
W. C., 38
William C., 49
CARVEN, Edward, 59
CASSART, David, 49
David S., 49

CASSAT, David, 22
Hannah F., 64
Jacob, 64
Sarah Y., 64
CATHCART, Rev., 30,
42, 43, 45, 49, 63, 64
Rev. Dr., 25, 27
Robert, 31
Sarah, 31
CAUDLE, Polly, 48
CAULL, Elizabeth, 27
CAVENAUGH, John,
57
CHAMBERS, William,
55
CHESTER, Elizabeth,
19
CHRISTINE, Jacob, 59,
62
Sarah, 59
CLARK, Lydia, 55
CLARKSON, Joseph, 51
Michael R., 12
Rev., 6, 25
Rev. Mr., 3
CLEMENT, Mary, 30
CLEMSON, Rev., 37
CLINGMAN, Jacob, 17
COADY, Sarah Ann, 60
COBEAN, Alexander,
17
Thomas B., 56
COLEMAN, James, 12
Robert, 12, 31, 32
Sarah Hand, 32
Susan, 7
COMFORT, Elizabeth,
15
CONN, George, 48
CONNELLY, Henry M.,

33
CONNOLLY, Ann, 6
Henry, 6, 45
Rachael, 45
CONRAD, John, 2
COOKE, Colin, 37
David, 22
COOKES, Daniel, 62
COOPER, Asenath Ann,
24
Cyrus, 24
Rebecca, 28
CORBEN, Eliza, 42
COTVIN, John H., 36
COULSTON, Sarah, 14
COULTER, William, 64
COVODE, John, 62
COWDEN, John, 39
COX, Henry, 8
John, 47
Joshua H., 40
Thomas, 40
CRABER, John, 20
Rev., 20
CRAMER, David, 18
Jacob, 51
Mary, 51
CRAVER, Rev., 7
Rev. Mr., 2
CREMER, Abraham, 1
Daniel, 57
Jacob, 57
Mary, 63
CRESLER, John, 43
CREVER, Rev., 7
CRISWELL, Ann, 18
Robert, 18
CROLL, John, 32
CRONE, Mary, 66
CROSS, George, 48

CROUT, John, 51
CULBERTSON, John,
19
William, 23
CUMFORT, Sarah, 48
CUNNINGHAM, John,
55
CURTIS, Dr., 26

-D-
DAHOFF, Rev., 9
DAILEY, Jacob, 61
DANNER, Abraham, 29,
41
Charlotte, 27, 41
George, 24
Martin, 27
Mary, 63
DARLINGTON,
Edward, 28
DASHIELL, George, 3
DAVIS, Abner, 59
Alcinda, 27
Phineas, 40
Rev., 27
Samuel, 12
DAWSON, Harriet, 12
DAY, Levi, 9
DECKER, Barbara, 6
Elizabeth, 8
Jacob, 8
DEHOFF, W. Bentz, 40
DEININGER, Rev., 63
DEISINGER, Barbara,
47
DELAMARE, Lewis, 13
DELLOW, Catherine,
28
DEMUTH, John, 19, 65
Sarah, 19

DE'PUI, John, 56
DESSENBERG, Peter, 61
DESSENBURGH,
 Anthony, 34
 Margaret, 34
DETWEILER, David, 18
DICK, Maria, 43
DICKEL, Peter, 8
DICKSON, William, 15
DIEHL, Charles, 4
 Daniel, 20
 George, 9
 Jacob, 4
 Nicholas, 7, 9
 Sarah, 7
DIETZ, Conrad, 56
 George, 11, 16
 Jacob, 21
DILL, Eleanor, 40
 John, 32
DILLINGER, Jacob, 45
DILLO, Henry, 29
DINGEE, Obadiah, 20
DINKLE, Peter, 47
DOBBINS, John, 3
 Margaret, 39
DOHM, Peter, 60
DOLB, Noah, 4
DOLL, Eliza, 20
 George F., 4
 Lydia, 40
DOM, Henry, 10
DOSCH, Christopher, 27
DOUDEL, Catharine, 8
 Helenah, 65
 Jacob, 8, 13
DOUGLASS, Elizabeth, 45

Rev., 37, 38, 54
DOWNEY, George, 3
DOWNS, Delila, 9
DRITT, Elizabeth, 20
 Jacob, 14, 36
 John, 14, 20
 Mrs., 36
DRORBAGH, Mary, 6
 Michael, 6
DUCHMAN, Jacob, 14
DUFF, James, 25
DUFFIELD, Philip, 53
 Rev., 26
 Rev. George, 59
DUNCAN, Andrew, 48
 Anna, 48
 Thomas, 47
DUNHAM, Thornton C., 65
DUNN, George, 23

-E-
EARICH, Mary, 15
EATEY, William, 14
EBERT, Daniel, 25
 Elisa Ann, 4
 Elizabeth, 44
 Matilda, 25
 Michael, 4
EDIE, David, 26
 John, 32
 Nancy, 26
EDWARDS, James, 34
EHRMAN, Catharine, 46
EICHELBERGER,
 Barnet, 57
 Eliza, 41
 Frederick, 6
 Jacob, 41

John, 2, 10, 15
 Juliana, 6
 Lydia, 10
 Martin, 62
 Miss, 55
 Sarah, 18, 57
 William, 32
EICHELBERHGER,
 Frederick, 18
EICHELEBERGER,
 George, 7
EICHHOLTZ,
 Elizabeth, 49
EISENHART,
 Catharine, 58
 George, 58
 Jacob, 28
ELLBY, John, 43
ELLIOT, Rev., 58
 Thomas, 27
EMIG, Anna Maria, 58
 Jacob, 53
 John, 58
 Margaret, 51
EMMETT, Susan, 9
ENDREAS, Rev., 3
ENDRESS, Rev., 35, 45
ENGLE, Rev., 10
EPLEY, Henry, 23
EPPLEY, Jacob, 4
 Joseph, 36
ERWIN, George, 2, 15
 Mary, 15
ESCHENBERG, John, 23
ETTER, Catharine, 33
 Samuel, 33
EURICH, Daniel, 48
 Michael, 36
EVANS, Ann, 49

Edward, 10
EVINGER, Jones G., 9
EYSTER, Elias, 56

-F-
FADDIS, Job H., 1
FAHNESTOCK, Borius,
    15
Henry, 14
John, 44
FAHS, Daniel, 49
Jacob, 46
John, 9
Lucinda, 27
Margaret, 46
FARQUHAR, Margaret,
    25
FARS, Mary, 26
FAUST, Baltzer, 42
Henry, 5
FEISER, Peter, 39
FELTENBERGER
Elizabeth, 48
Henry, 48
FELTY, Jacob, 34
FERREE, Andrew, 53
Catharine, 53
Mrs., 53
FIDLER, Joseph, 10
FILBY, Rebecca, 62
FINDLAY, William S., 5
FINDLEY, William, 2
FINFROCK, George, 35
Philip, 35
FISCHER, Catharine, 4
John, 4
FISHER, Catharine, 4
David, 20
Eliza, 30
Elizabeth, 2

George, 2, 54
John, 4, 30
Lewis, 1
Nancy, 20
FISSEL, Ann Maria, 64
FITZ, Jane, 35
FLINT, Robert, 49
FORBES, Elizabeth, 21
FORD, Mrs., 10
FORNEY, Adam, 10
Elizabeth, 19
Rebecca, 24
Samuel, 19
Susan, 21
FORRY, Elizabeth, 20
Rudolph, 20
FORSTER, Margaret,
    12
FORTENBACH,
    Andrew, 16
FORTENBOUGH,
    Andrew, 13
FOULERL, Benjamin, 2
FRANK, Elizabeth, 58
FRANKEBERGER,
    Philip, 5
FRANKLIN, Mary, 16
W., 16
Walter S., 6
FRAZER, James G., 63
FREE, Peter, 43
FREEMAN, Susanna,
    43
FREET, Jacob, 4
FREY, Adam, 45
Elizabeth, 42
George, 50
Jacob, 45
Louisa, 37
Mary, 42

FRIE, John, 5
Mrs., 5
FRIESS, Lydia, 53
FRITZ, Juliana, 52
FRY, Elizabeth, 9
Peter, 9
Rev. Joseph, 60
FULLERTON, Robert,
    66
FUNK, Joseph, 13
FURNACE, Margaretta,
    48
FURRELL, Ann, 64
FURRY, Margaret, 28
Rudolph, 28

-G-
GABRIEL, Elizabeth,
    30
GARBER, Mara, 8
GARDNER, Margaret,
    21
Martin, 21
GARRETSON,
    Cornelius, 57
Rev. Aquilla, 2
Samuel, 11
GARTNER, Israel, 25
Jacob, 33
GATES, Elizabeth, 2
John, 48
GEESY, Michael, 14
GEISTWEIT, Rev., 9,
    11, 35, 38, 40, 43
GEMMILL, Mary, 42
Robert, 42
GIBSON, James, 37
Susanna, 37
GILCHELL, Margaret,
    15

GILLESPY, Nathaniel, 28
GILMORE, Sarah, 45
GINTER, Henry, 61
Jacob, 28
GIPE, Mary, 50
GLATZ, Jacob, 51
GLENN, Eliza, 62
Rebecca, 59
William, 59
GOFOTH, Rev., 59
GOOD, Catharine, 53
GOODRIDGE, William, 37
GOODYEAR, Charles, 30
GORDON, Hannah, 34
GOSSLER, Philip, 4
GOTTWALT, Catharine, 35
Henry, 31
Mrs., 5
GOTWALT, Sarah, 56
GRAEFF, Christian, 11
Jacob, 8
GRAFFIUS, Abraham, 7, 65
Catharine, 7
GRAHAM, John, 26
GRANGER, Gideon, 15
GRATZ, Jesse, 11
GRAVER, George, 62
GRAYBILL, Jacob, 25
Michael, 25
GREEN, Clementine, 61
Elisha, 3
GREER, Ann, 44
Robert, 44
GRIER, Rev., 40
Robert, 33

GRIFFITH, Phebe, 62
William, 56
GRIGGS, James M., 58
GRIMES, Margaret, 55
GROSS, Daniel, 7
Elizabeth, 7
Henry, 45
GROVE, Isaac, 53
John, 47
Mathew, 42
Samuel, 9
GUNDACKER, Catherine, 28
GUTELIUS, Samuel, 26
GUY, John, 37
Mary, 37

-H-
HABBELSTEIN, Rev., 3
HABLESTON, Rev., 10
HABLISTON, Rev., 10, 11, 13, 14, 20
Rev. Henry, 4, 9
HAHN, Ann, 25
John, 25
HAIL, Rev., 37
HAKE, John, 55
HALL, Charles, 1
Rev., 44, 50
Richard D., 56
HALLER, George, 4
John, 24
HALLOWELL, Benjamin, 25
Elisha, 54
HAMAKER, Ann, 24
Christian, 24
HAMERSLEY, R., 39
HAMERSLY, H., 39

Juliet M., 44
Pamela, 24
R., 44, 47
Robert, 24
HAMILTON, Judge, 23
Susan, 23
HAMME, Jonas, 58
HAMMER, Elizabeth, 59
HAMMOND, Henry, 14
HANIS, Catharine, 47
HANNEWALT, John, 34
HANTZ, Emanuel H., 35
Jacob, 7, 35
HARD, Ovid, 13
HARDT, Peter, 1
HARLAN, Amelia, 23
Joseph, 23
HARMAN, Abraham, 27
Margaret, 62
HARPER, Louisa, 12
Robert, 12
HARRY, Margaret, 27
Reuben, 19
Stephen, 27
HART, John, 11
Sarah, 11
HAUGHMAN, Elizabeth, 28
HAY, Eliza, 46
George, 13, 62
Henry, 38
Jacob, 7, 46
John, 7, 18
Julia, 13
Michael, 17
Sarah, 62
William, 18

HAYES, Mary, 17
HAYS, Jane, 59
Joseph, 59
Mills, 27
Mrs., 56
HECKART, Jacob, 52
HECKERT, Cassandra, 7
Charles, 45
Daniel, 28
HECKERY, Sarah, 34
HECKMAN, William, 52
HEINDEL, George, 61
HEITSHUE, Daniel, 44
Mary, 44
HEKCERT, Daniel, 63
HELFFENSTEIN, Rev., 21
HELMBOLDT, George, 6
HELMUTH, Rev. Dr., 27
HELTENSTEIN, Rev., 31
HELTZE, Lydia, 11
HEMPHILL, Joseph, 1
Rev., 43, 46, 48
HENDERSON, Thomas, 62
HENDRIX, Eli, 19
HENRY, Adam, 35
Caroline M., 33
George, 20
Jane, 36
Joseph, 36
Judge, 33
HENSHAW, Rev., 62
HEPBURN, Sarah, 39
HERBAUGH, Jacob, 43
Sarah, 43

HERBST, Rev., 41
Rev. John, 3
HERMAN, Andrew, 34
David, 35
Lydia, 21
HERSH, John, 3, 26
Mary, 3
HERSHEY, Lena, 7
HERSHY, Barbara, 63
Mary, 52
Susanna, 52
HESS, Abraham, 61
HETTSHU, Daniel, 36
HIBNER, Frederick, 52
HIDEBRAND,
Catharine Christiana, 38
Christian, 38
Sarah, 38
HIESTAND, Abraham, 12, 25, 37, 51, 61
Elizabeth, 12
John, 18
Nancy, 25, 37
Susan, 51
HIESTER, Elizabeth, 29
Joseph, 29
HILDEBRAND,
Caroline Louisa, 40
Christian, 22, 40, 56
HINCKLEY, Jacob, 60
HINES, Anthony, 54
HINKLE, George W., 39
HISS, Charlotte, 47
HOFFMAN, Catherine, 30
HOFFMEIER, Charles F., 38

HOHENLOHE, Prince, 21
HOKE, Eliza, 5
Frederick, 45
George, 52
Jacob, 1, 5
Lydia, 45
Peter, 5, 9, 57
HOMMER, Mary, 22
HOOD, Rev., 39
HOOVER, John, 28
HOPKINS, George R., 1
James, 1
Mr., 46
Samuel, 62
Washington, 16
HORN, John, 62
HOUGH, Jonathan, 49
Samuel, 49
HOUSEMAN, Mrs., 30
HUBLEY, Arah, 31
HUGH, Samuel H., 28
HUNTER, Rachael, 64
HUTTER, Henry A., 21
HUTTON, Martha, 54
Thomas, 50
HUVNER, Elizabeth, 33
HYDE, David, 55

-I-
IAWIN, John, 13
ILGENFRITZ,
Abraham, 58
Ann, 47
Elizabeth, 1
George, 48, 51
Henry, 44
Jacob, 26
Lenah, 42
Margaret, 44

Maria, 26
Samuel, 1, 9, 42, 47, 65
Sarah, 51
Susan, 9
IMFELT, Lydia, 42
INGLES, Thomas, 4
INNERST, Lydia, 23
IRWIN, Patrick, 8

-J-
JACKSON, Daniel, 37
Maria, 46
Mrs., 8
Samuel, 54
JACOBS, Ann Maria, 63
George, 19, 50
Jacob, 55
James A., 7
Rebecca, 19
Wilson, 63
JAMES, Harriett, 50
Mary, 25
Nicholas, 50
JAMESON, Catherine, 20
Thomas, 20
JEFFERSON, Delia, 37
JEFFRIES, Caroline, 18
Harriet, 14
Joseph, 14, 25
JESSOP, Jonathan, 29
Susan, 29
JOHNS, Rev., 36, 49
JOHNSON, Eliza, 36
Peter, 11
Roger, 36
William, 52
JOHNSTON, James, 55

Rachel, 15
Samuel, 62
William, 15
JONES, Elizabeth, 33
Emma, 15
Mary, 43
Robert, 11, 15, 33
JORDAN, Samuel, 52
William, 13

-K-
KALKGRESSER, John, 6
KALTREITER, Jacob, 11
KARBER, Christiana, 43
George, 43
KAUFFMAN, Christiana, 16
Daniel, 65
Jacob, 16
Lydia, 57
KAUFMAN, John, 4, 43
John H., 62
Mary, 4, 8
Samuel, 9
KEEFER, Jacob, 62
John, 59
Lewis, 45
KEISER, Sarah, 23
KELLER, John Jacob, 64
Rev., 46
KELLEY, Elizabeth, 62
James, 62
KELLY, Carvel, 45
Eben S., 56
Esamiah, 20
James, 45

John, 20, 26
John J., 1
Margaret, 26
KENDALL, Moses, 37
KENDRICK, Prudence, 14
KENDRICKS, Miss, 52
KENNERLY, Rev. Samuel, 27
KEPLAR, Rev., 63
KERN, Frederick, 48
Magdalene, 48
KERR, Catharine, 41
Rev. William, 6
KESHER, Rev. J. R., 63
KINDER, John, 58
KINDIG, Jacob, 35
Mrs., 44
KING, Barbar, 54
Catharine, 7
Catherine, 33
George, 15
Julia Ann, 31
Nancy, 25
Philip J., 31, 33, 54, 56
KIRK, Eli, 46
Hannah, 22
Isaac, 5, 39, 60, 62, 65
Jacob, 22, 23
John, 5
KIRKWOOD, Robert, 7
KISTER, Adam, 3
KLATFELTER, Maria, 49
KLEINFELTER, Lawrence, 65
KLINE, George W., 16
Henry, 15
Peter, 7
KLINEDIENST, David,

43
KLINEFELTER, Adam,
53
Catharine, 53
Elizabeth, 22
Eve, 45
Michael, 22
KLUGE, Henrietta, 54
J. P., 47, 50, 54, 55,
59, 62, 63
Mrs., 47
Rev., 49, 51, 57
KLUGEY, Rev., 44
KNAB, Casper, 21
Miss, 21
KNAUB, Magdalene, 7
KNOH, Francis, 37
KOCH, Elizabeth, 33
Francis, 33
KOCHENOUR, Henry,
30
KOCK, Frederick, 17
KOENIGMUCHER,
Adam, 1
KOON, Francis, 12
KOONS, Elizabeth, 32
Francis, 32
Francis L., 28
John, 29
Michael, 4
Samuel, 29
Spangler, 55
KOSEL, Margaret, 26
KOTH, Margaret, 48
Richard, 48
KOTTER, Jacob, 16
KRABER, Catharine, 52
J. G. 53
Martin, 56
Rev., 36, 52

KRAMLIN, Jacob, 14
KREBER, Rev., 8, 47
KREIDLER, Christian,
23
KREPPER, William, 58
KRIBER, Rev., 35
KROAN, Lawrence, 16
KROHN, Leah, 60
KRONE, John, 35
Lydia, 46
KROUSE, William, 51
KURTZ, Benjamin, 41
Caroline E., 41
Charles, 6, 53
George P., 30
Jacob, 2
Sarah A., 2

-L-
LAMOTT, David, 64
LANDIS, Daniel, 62
John, 11
Mrs., 62
Susan, 51
LANDT, Catharine, 35
Peter, 35
LANIUS, Amelia, 44
Benjamin, 1
Christian, 23, 44
Eliza, 23
LANSINGER, John, 30
LATIMER, George, 29
LATTIMER, Sarah, 12
William, 12
LATTMER, James, 31
LAUB, Sarah, 27
William, 21
LAUKS, A. M., 45
Jacob, 45, 53
LAUMAN, Charles, 11

LAUMASTER,
Catherine, 26
Charles, 20
Eliza, 41
LAYMAN, Mary, 7
LEAS, George, 18
LEDBER, Samuel, 11
LEFEVRE, Jacob, 40
LEFFLER, Rev., 9, 12,
14, 15, 20, 21, 23, 25,
26, 27, 28, 31, 37, 38,
40, 41, 44
LEHMAN, Daniel, 46
Dr. William, 56
LEHR, Casper, 29
John, 54, 60
Margaret, 60
LEINAWEAVER,
Catharine, 16
Peter, 16
LEITNER, George, 1,
52
Ignatius, 52
Mary, 1
LENHART, Elizabeth,
43
Godfrey, 22
Maria Elizabeth, 22
Rev. John, 59
LETH, Joseph, 9
LEWIS, Eli, 24
Elizabth, 45
Ellis, 13, 45
Rebecca, 35
Webster, 35
LICHTY, Elizabeth, 48
LIEBENSTEIN,
George, 50
Jacob, 64
LIEBERKNECHT,

George, 8
LIEBHART, Elizabeth, 37
Jacob, 37
LIFE, Robert, 9
LINDT, Mrs., 34
Peter, 34
LINTON, William, 30
LIST, Lydia, 28
Peter, 12
LITTEL, James, 56
LLOYD, George, 50
LOCHMAN, George, 38
Rev., 18, 26, 27
Rev. Dr., 20
LOCHNER, Catharine, 53
LOEHMAN, Augustus H., 31
LOGAN, Henry, 27
LONENECKER, Leah, 61
LONG, Mary, 16
LONIUS, Barbara, 3
LOUCKS, Elizabeth, 57
George, 2
LOW, John, 10
LOWRY, Robert K., 34
LUCKY, Rev., 7
LUNNAN, Thomas, 17
LUTES, Jane, 62
LUTMAN, Elizabeth, 50
LUTTMAN, George, 7, 24
John, 4
Leah, 4
Mrs., 24
LUTZ, Elizabeth, 27
LUUMAN, Susan, 15
LYNCH, Miss., 40

LYON, Matthew, 13

-M-
M'ALLEN, Catharine, 34
MCALLISTER, Eleanor, 32
James, 32
MCARTHUR, Mary, 37
MCCAHON, Alexander, 63
M'CALMOND, Jane, 64
MCCANN, Peter, 36
Polly, 36
M'CLEAN, Archibald, 12
MCCLELLAN, William, 3
M'CONAUGHY, Rev., 26
Rev. D., 64
MCDONOUGH, Commodore, 32
M'FULL, James, 4
MCGREW, Jane, 4
M'GUIRE, Peter, 63
Ruth, 43
Sarah, 63
MACHLIN, Rebecca, 11
M'ILHENNY, James, 64
Samuel, 64
MCISHEIMER, Rev., 12, 24, 35
MCKENZIE, Jane, 41
M'KNIGHT, John, 40
Sarah, 40
M'MILLEN, George, 39
MCMUNN, Robert, 38
M'MUNN, William, 33
MCPHERSON, Joseph, 64

MANIFOLD, John, 49
MANN, John, 51, 63
MANX, Sally, 38
MARKEY, John, 50
MARKS, William, 63
MARTIN, Christian, 27
John, 34
MATHEWS, Margaret, 10
Rev., 65
MATTHIAS, George, 60
MAXWELL, Matilda, 39
Susan B., 58
William, 58
MAY, Catharine, 60
MAYER, Catherine Amelia, 33
Christian Henutz, 33
Col., 14
David, 28
Henry, 63
John Jacob, 48
Lewis, 45
Louis, 33
Louis Henry, 33
Margaret, 3
Rev., 9, 10, 13, 15, 16, 18, 19, 21, 24, 25, 27, 28, 65
Rev. Mr., 1
Virginia, 33
MEADS, Benedict, 49
Miranda, 49
MELGINGER, Englehardt, 7
MELSHEIMER, Charles, 31
Ferdinand A., 49
Rev., 14, 16, 19, 39

John F., 55
MELSHEINER, Rev.,
 11
MENGES, George, 51
MENGST, George, 40
MEREDITH, Hannah,
 23
MERRILL, James, 29,
 39
 Mary, 29
METZEL, Eliza, 4
METZGAR, John, 3
 Samuel, 42
 William, 18
METZGER, Paul, 42
MEYER, Jacob, 32
 John, 59
MEYERHEFFER, Rev.,
 32
MEYERS, Abdiel, 5
 David, 5
 Jane, 39
 Jesse, 5
 John, 40
 Jonas, 38
 Rev., 7
MICHAEL, Mary, 42
 Miss, 15
 William, 31
MIFFLIN, Samuel, 56
MILLARD, Abigail, 5
 Samuel, 5
MILLER, Abraham, 29,
 59
 Adam, 8
 Ananias, 44
 Andrew, 62, 11
 Andrew G., 41
 Catharine, 11
 Catherine, 13

Christian, 37, 44, 50
Constantius, 2, 5
 David, 2, 62
 Elizabeth, 6
 Henry, 6, 17, 18, 21,
 62
 James, 36
 John, 8, 34
 Leah, 26
 Lydia, 58
 Mrs., 50
 Rev. Mr., 1
 Robert, 36
 Rudolph, 12
 Sarah, 18
 Susan, 34
MINICH, Catharine, 14
 Jonathan, 14
MINNICH, George, 44
 Jacob, 42
 Leah, 41
 Matilda, 49
 Simon, 41, 49
MONTGOMERY,
 William, 33
MOORE, Ann, 2
 Gertrude, 48
 L., 64
 Peter E., 48, 54
MORRIS, John, 15
 John G., 46
 Joseph, 63
 Mary, 41
 Robert, 41
MORRISON, John, 27
 Margaret, 27
 Michael, 27
 Mr., 59
MORTHLAND,
 Rebecca, 39, 61

MORX, Jacob, 11
 Mrs., 11
MOSEY, Catharine, 19
 John, 19, 35
 Mary, 35
MOYER, Rev., 14
MUHLENBERG, Rev.,
 16
MUNDORF, Samuel, 27
MUNTIS, George, 21
 Susan, 21
MURRAY, Lindsey, 36
MUSSELMAN, Eliza,
 51
MYER, Louisa W., 49
 Philip, 53
 Sarah Christiana, 48
 Solomon, 49
MYERS, Benjamin, 48
 David, 11
 Henry, 32
 John, 48, 65
 Rev., 35

-N-
NAGGLE, Jacob, 59
NAILOR, Mary, 63
NARR, Elisa H., 31
NEELY, James L., 64
 John, 64
NEFF, Rebecca, 30
NELL, Jacob, 43
NELLINGER,
 Magdalena, 41
NES, John, 23
 William, 47
NEUMAN, Andrew, 54
NEVINS, George P., 47
NEWMAN, Andres, 26
 Andrew, 18

Sarah, 26
NICHOLAS, John, 63
NICHOLS, James, 60
William, 39
NICHOLSON, Mr., 43
NORRIS, Mrs., 36
William, 36

-O-
OBERHOLTZER,
Elizabeth, 45
ODENWALT, John, 13
O'HAIL, Martha, 27
ORRICK, Davenport, 40
Samuel D., 3
OSWALD, J., 61, 65
OVERDOFF, George,
43

-P-
PALMER, Elizabeth
Margaretta, 46
John B., 46
PARSON, Abner, 21
PARTENHEIMER,
Adam, 31
Anna Maria, 31
PATTERSON, James,
19
PATTON, Maria, 55
PEARCE, Rev., 27
PEARSON, Sarah Ann,
64
PENFIELD, Isabella, 34
PENROSE, Charles B.,
21
PENTZ, Joanna, 60
John, 22, 35
Matilda, 22
PETER, Elizabeth, 53

George Michael, 29
PETERS, William, 40
PETRY, Elizabeth, 62
PETSEL, Abraham, 63
Catharine, 63
PFLIEFER, George, 2
PFLIEGER, Jacob, 60
PHILLIPS, George, 22
PHLEEGER, Henry, 48
PIERCE, Susanna, 57
PLATTS, Elizabth, 64
Thomas, 64
POCHON, Charles
Julian Joseph, 54
POOR, Ann, 59
George, 3
John, 65
PORTER, James, 61
Martha, 61
POTTS, Abegail, 58
Nathan, 6
PRESTON, John, 1
PRETTYMAN, William,
16
PRICE, George, 6
PRINCE, David B., 25
PRINGLE, Rev., 27
PUTNAM, Rufus, 22

-R-
RAHAUSER, Rev., 12
RAMSAY, Samuel, 37
William D., 50
RANDALS, Tommy, 51
RANDOLPH, Thomas,
51
RATHFONG, Christian,
25
RAUFENBERGER,
Christian, 13

RAYMER, Henry, 53
REAMAN, John, 16
REES, Abraham, 30
REESE, Catharine, 35
Mary, 50
William, 35
REICHART, Hannah,
24
REIGART, Wilhelmina,
11
REILY, J. R., 50, 51, 52,
53, 54, 58, 59, 61, 63
Rev., 43, 45, 47, 48,
49, 50, 62, 65
REINOLL, Daniel, 54
REISINGER,
Alexander, 56
Henry, 53
Mary, 57
REITZEL, John, 38
REITZELL, Henry, 33
RENSEL, John, 55
Rebecca, 55
REYNOLDS, Catharine,
14, 53
RICHMOND, Rhoda
Mason, 28
William, 28
RINGGOLD, Ann S., 3
RITTER, Andrew, 22
RODE, John, 44
RODNEY, Caesar A., 23
Eliza, 23
ROEMER, Elizabeth, 50
ROFFINGSBERGER,
John, 53
ROGERS, Abraham, 23
Mary, 23
ROMAN, Cordelia, 43
ROSENBAUM, John,

17
ROSS, Alexander, 27
Caroline, 3
Elizabeth, 27
George, 3
Hugh, 59
Robert, 11
ROTH, Abraham, 35
Christian, 52
ROUSE, Luke, 3
Elizabeth, 16
John, 10, 16
Samuel, 10
RUBY, Joseph, 65
Julian, 58
Peter, 61
RUDISELL, Eliza, 46
RUDY, George, 15, 34
Jacob, 26
Magdalena, 34
Sarah Ann, 26
Susan, 13
RUFF, Louisa, 49
RUNK, Ann, 59
RUPP, Christian, 6
Peter, 29
RUSSEL, Ann, 32
RUTTER, Andrew, 37
RYDE, Samuel, 53

-S-
SANDERSON, Samuel,
44
Sarah, 44
SANDOE, Maria, 61
SAYLOR, Mary, 51
SCANLAN, James, 52
SCHAEFFER, George
B., 33
Rev., 8

SCHAFER, Jacob, 55
SCHALL, Thomas B.,
61
SCHECKLES, Mary, 59
SCHEFFER, Henry, 47
SCHLATTER, William,
41
SCHLOSSER, Hannah,
43
Jacob, 26
John, 43
Sarah, 24
SCHMELTZER,
Elizabeth, 60
SCHMIDT, Joseph W.,
21
SCHMUCK, Joseph, 56
SCHMUCKER, D., 64
Eleanora, 18
Eliza, 28
J. G., 28
Rev., 6, 7, 8, 12, 13,
15, 16, 17, 19, 20, 22,
23, 24, 25, 26, 28, 30,
31, 35, 36, 37, 39, 41,
42, 44, 46, 51, 53, 54,
56, 57, 61, 64, 65
Rev. Mr., 1, 2, 4
Samuel, 18
Samuel S., 32
SCHOLL, Susan, 14
SCHRIVER, Margaret,
56
Sarah, 11
SCHROCK, John, 23
SCHROEDER, Emanuel
H., 41, 58
Leah, 58
SCHROLL, John, 54
SCHULLY, Isabella, 19

SCHULTZ, Jacob, 1
Marriet, 35
Samuel, 54
SCHULUZE, John
Andrew, 15
Mary, 15
SCHWARTZ, David, 55
SCOTT, John, 6
SCUDDER, Daniel, 55
SEARS, Peter, 10
SEDGEWICK, Sarah,
25
SEIFERT, Rev., 34
SHAEFFER, Elizabeth,
17
Rev., 39
Sarah, 11
SHAFER, Frederick, 59
SHAFFNER, Rev. H.
B., 37
SHANK, Catharine, 2
George, 2
John, 40
SHARBONE, Mr., 36
SHARER, George, 41
SHARP, Mary, 39
SHARRETTE, Nicholas,
46
SHE (?), Louisa, 65
SHELLY, John, 18, 21
Susan, 18
SHENBERGER, Adam,
12
SHENFELTER,
George, 23
SHEPHERD, Jacob, 62
SHERMAN, Conrad, 17
Jacob, 17
SHETTER, Elizabeth,
30

George, 30
Martin, 59
Mrs., 59
SHETTLEY, Cassandra, 44
SHIRE, David, 37
Mary, 37
SHOCH, J. G., 63
SHONK, Barbara, 55
SHRAMM, Catharine, 6
SHRIVER, Elizabeth, 26
James, 26
SHUE, Catharine, 9
Michael, 14
SHUFF, John, 46
Salome, 46
SHULTZ, David, 19
Jacob, 57
Lorentz, 29
Peter, 35, 50
Sarah, 35
SHULZE, George, 42
John A., 18
SHUNK, William, 30
SIMS, Francis, 60
SLAGLE, William, 60
SLEEGER, Daniel, 25
SMALL, Anna Mary, 26
Daniel, 2
Geo., 12
Henry, 19
Jacob, 15
John, 46
Joseph, 14
Margaret Maria, 16
Mrs., 2
Peter, 16, 17
Philip, 12
William, 39

SMITH, Anne, 38
Charles, 13
Chester, 5
Daniel, 15
Elizabeth, 45, 56
George, 10
John, 10, 21, 42, 61
Joseph, 25
Lewis, 65
Margaret, 53
Maria, 45, 61
Mary, 5
Mrs., 25
Rebecca, 58
Rev., 57, 62, 63, 64
Robert, 10, 13, 61
Samuel, 19, 27
Thomas, 36
Thomas Jefferson, 49
SMYSER, Adam, 60
Anna Myra, 34
Daniel, 59
Eliza, 16
Israel, 25
Jacob, 16, 48
Louisa, 48
Lydia, 16
Mary, 59, 62
Matthias, 55, 57
Michael, 16, 34, 62
Peter, 50
Sarah, 50, 60
William, 63
SNOWDEN, N.R., 7
SNYDER, Catharine, 10, 21
Eliza, 20
Henry, 56
SNYSER, Michael, 23
SOLOMON, George, 49

SOUR, Casper, 37
SOWER, Casper, 29
Catherine, 29
SPANGLER, Ann, 31
Anna Mary, 34
Baltzer, 4, 17, 39
Charles, 35
Charlotte, 28
Christina, 4
Daniel, 12, 31, 41
Eliza, 1, 61
Elizabeth, 20
Emanuel, 28
Ferdinand L., 61
George, 17, 28
George W., 41, 58
Jacob, 51
Jesse, 28, 50, 55
Louisa, 50
Lydia, 55
Margaret, 12
Mary Ann, 28
Peter, 17, 20
Rudolph, 17, 43
Samuel, 1, 5, 11, 25, 48, 58
Washington, 25
William, 34
SPANGLERD, Jonas, 5
SPECK, Rev. Mr., 2
SPEER, Alexander, 49
James, 39
Mary, 49
SPENCER, Mary, 65
SPOTTSWOOD, Lindsey, 46
Louise, 46
SPRENKLE, Catherine, 35
Mary, 2

Mrs., 20
Peter, 15
SPRIGG, Rev., 58
STAIR, Ann Maria, 61
STALL, John, 45
STARK, Ezra P., 8
STAUGH, Peter, 7
STAUTER, John, 19
STAVELY, Christian, 12
STECHER, Rev., 16
STECHMAN, Rev., 11
STECKER, Rev., 57
STEEN, John, 30
STEENBERGEN, Mary Catherine, 32
W., 32
STEINER, Mary Ann, 18
STERUITT, Julianna, 10
STEVENS, Thomas, 65
STEVENSON, W., 2
STEWART, John, 9
Mary, 50
Mrs., 9
STICKEL, Peter, 14
STILLINGER, Charles, 35
STOCKDALE, John, 2
STODDART, Christopher, 5
STOEHR, Barbara, 13
Christopher, 4
STONER, Lydia, 12
Pennington, 28
STOOPS, Mary, 53
STRAPP, Mr., 65
STRAYER, Samuel, 47
STREBER, William, 9

STREHER, Adam, 14
Maria, 14
STRICKLAND, Joseph, 7
STRICKLER, Jacob, 10, 58
Mary, 10
STROMAN, Henry, 27
Jacob, 15
John, 6
Mrs., 27
STROUSE, Adam, 39
STUART, John, 34
Maria, 32
STUCK, Jacob, 54
STUMP, Eliza, 2
Susan, 40
STURGEON, William, 12
SULSBACH, Elizabeth, 18
Henry, 18
SUMMERS, Rebecca, 63
SUMMY, John, 43
SURGER, Charles, 24
SWARTZBACH, Catharine, 65

-T-
TAYLOR, Cornelia, 24
Hannah, 40
Jany, 19
Joseph, 44
Nicholas W., 40
Thomas, 40
TEISTWERT, Rev., 41
TEKLODT, William, 61
TEST, John, 25, 29
Mary, 29

THOMAS, Hannah, 25
Nathan, 10
THOMPSON, Charles, 24
Elizabeth, 7
Samuel, 60
THORNE, John, 23
TIDINGS, Rev., 34
TILGHMAN, William, 43
TIPTON, Ruth, 51
TOBERT, Rev., 16
TODD, James, 18, 35
Joseph, 18
TRACEY, Josiah, 64
TREXLER, Jeremiah, 51
TRIVER, Jacob, 10
TRUETT, John, 53
Sarah, 53
TRUITT, John, 34
TURBUTT, Maria, 39
Nicholas, 39
TURK, Sarah, 60
TURNER, Alexander, 43
Mary, 43
TYDINGS, Rev., 3
TYLER, Catharine, 58
TYSON, Daniel, 59
Jacob, 11

-U-
UPDEGRAPH, Eli, 29
UPP, Ann, 47
George, 44
Jacob, 31, 47
Julia, 44

-V-
VAN VLECK, Rev., 12
VANNARD, William, 32
VINTON, Rev., 9, 11,
16, 26
VOGLESONG, John, 34
VONDERSLOODT, F.
W., 55
VONDERSLOTH, Rev.,
43

-W-
WADSWORTH,
Manning, 66
WAGNER, Catharine,
28
George, 19
John, 42
Polly, 9
Samuel, 42
William, 12
WALES, Mary, 14
William, 14
WALL, Jacob, 3
John, 3
Nancy, 3
WALLACE, Evelina, 37
Josephine, 13
WALLS, Ephraim, 41
WALTEMEYER, Eliza,
14
Philip, 60
WALTMAN, Daniel, 30
WAMPLER, Daniel, 22
Joseph, 8
Mrs., 8
Sarah, 15
WANBAGH, Harriet, 6
John, 6
WANBAUCH, John, 21

WANBAUGH, William,
26
WARNER, Catharine,
10
WASHINGTON, Anne,
64
Hon. Bushrod, 64
WEARLEY, Charlotte,
51
WEAVER, Catharine,
57
Daniel, 57
WEBB, George, 60
Joseph W., 54
WEBSTER, Hosea, 25
WEHLHAF, Mary, 48
WEIGEL, Margaret, 62
WEISER, Daniel B., 22
Daniel P., 20
Eliza, 65
Henry, 51
Margaret, 38
Maria Catharine, 10
Martin, 10
Martin J., 63
Mary, 36
Samuel, 7, 36, 38, 44,
47, 65
Susan, 36
WEITZEL, John, 20
WELSH, Barbara, 34
Catharine, 21
Catherine, 25
Charles, 34, 41
George, 35
Hannah, 20, 42
Henry, 16
John, 21, 64
Michael, 25
Rebecca, 64

William, 20, 42
WELTY, Anna Maria,
61
WENTZ, Elizabth, 35
Mr., 35
WESTHEFFER, Peter,
61
WETHERILL, Charles,
3
WHITE, Rev. Bishop,
12
WHITT, Bishop, 41
WIEMER, Andrew, 9
Catharine, 9
WIESER, Martin, 13
WIESTLING, Rev., 19
J. H., 7, 8
WILDIE, Jacob, 20
WILEY, Joseph, 26
WILL, Eveline, 8
Jacob, 8
Rebecca, 50
WILLHELM, Daniel, 37
WILLIAMS, Eliza, 64
John, 55
John F., 64
Mr., 48
Rev., 23, 25
WILLIAMSON, Rev.,
36, 43, 63
WILLING, Thomas, 1
Thomas M., 13
WILLIS, Hannah, 3
John, 3
Margaret L., 60
WILSON, A., 38
Catharine, 37
Charles, 10
David, 62
Eliza, 65

Joshiah, 38
Rev., 21
WILT, Charlotte, 27
Jacob, 42
Miss, 35
Peter, 35
V., 27
WINDER, William H.,
22
WINEBRENNER,
Catherine, 32
George, 63
Rev., 10
WINEHOLDT, Harriet,
55
Leah, 61
WINKS, Elizabeth, 13
WIRT, Christian, 39
Deliah, 39
WIRTZ, Eliza, 9
WITMER, John, 35
WOLF, Adam, 32
Israel, 44
WOLFF, John, 57
Lydia, 57
WORLEY, Abigail, 21
Francis, 42
James, 21
John, 19, 44
Joseph, 65
Louisa, 65
Margaret, 17
Nathan, 16, 19
WRIGHT, Charles N.,
40
Delia Amanda, 61
Ebenezer, 57, 61
John L., 49
WYETH, Francis, 58
-Y-

YESLER, Henry, 24
Margaret, 24
YESSLEN, Catharine,
54
YOCUM, William, 27
YOUNG, Daniel, 63
Dr. Henry, 42
George, 14
YOUSE, John, 15

-Z-
ZACHARIAS, Peter, 54
Rev., 55, 58, 60
Rev. D., 59, 60, 61, 63
Rev. Daniel, 59
ZEIGLER, Catherine,
20
John, 20
ZELLARS, Rosanna, 61
ZIEGEL, Elizabeth, 5
Thomas, 5
ZIEGLER, Benjamin, 46
George, 38
George P., 42
Martin, 22
Peter, 45
Susanna, 45
ZINK, Samuel, 65
ZINN, Mrs., 37
ZOEGER, Frederick, 9
ZORGER, Ann, 51

Marriages and Deaths in the Newspapers of Lancaster County, Pennsylvania, 1821-1830

Marriages and Deaths in the Newspapers of Lancaster County, Pennsylvania, 1831-1840

Marriages and Deaths of Cumberland County, [Pennsylvania], 1821-1830

Maryland Calendar of Wills Volume 9: 1744-1749

Maryland Calendar of Wills Volume 10: 1748-1753

Maryland Calendar of Wills Volume 11: 1753-1760

Maryland Calendar of Wills Volume 12: 1759-1764

Maryland Calendar of Wills Volume 13: 1764-1767

Maryland Calendar of Wills Volume 14: 1767-1772

Maryland Calendar of Wills Volume 15: 1772-1774

Maryland Calendar of Wills Volume 16: 1774-1777

Maryland Eastern Shore Newspaper Abstracts, Volume 1: 1790-1805

Maryland Eastern Shore Newspaper Abstracts, Volume 2: 1806-1812

Maryland Eastern Shore Newspaper Abstracts, Volume 3: 1813-1818

Maryland Eastern Shore Newspaper Abstracts, Volume 4: 1819-1824

Maryland Eastern Shore Newspaper Abstracts, Volume 5: Northern Counties, 1825-1829
F. Edward Wright and Irma Harper

Maryland Eastern Shore Newspaper Abstracts, Volume 6: Southern Counties, 1825-1829

Maryland Eastern Shore Newspaper Abstracts, Volume 7: Northern Counties, 1830-1834
Irma Harper and F. Edward Wright

Maryland Eastern Shore Newspaper Abstracts, Volume 8: Southern Counties, 1830-1834

Maryland Militia in the Revolutionary War
S. Eugene Clements and F. Edward Wright

Newspaper Abstracts of Allegany and Washington Counties, Maryland, 1811-1815

Newspaper Abstracts of Cecil and Harford Counties, Maryland, 1822-1830

Newspaper Abstracts of Frederick County, Maryland, 1816-1819

Newspaper Abstracts of Frederick County, Maryland, 1811-1815

Sketches of Maryland Eastern Shoremen

Tax List of Chester County, Pennsylvania 1768

Tax List of York County, Pennsylvania 1779

Washington County Church Records of the 18th Century, 1768-1800

Western Maryland Newspaper Abstracts, Volume 1: 1786-1798

Western Maryland Newspaper Abstracts, Volume 2: 1799-1805

Western Maryland Newspaper Abstracts, Volume 3: 1806-1810

Wills of Chester County, Pennsylvania, 1766-1778

www.ingramcontent.com/pod-product-compliance
Lightning Source LLC
LaVergne TN
LVHW051704080426
835511LV00017B/2719